*Love,
Death,
and the
Changing
of the
Seasons*

BY MARILYN HACKER

Winter Numbers

Going Back to the River

Love, Death, and the Changing of the Seasons

Assumptions

Taking Notice

Separations

Presentation Piece

Selected Poems 1965–1990

Squares and Courtyards

Love, Death, and the Changing of the Seasons

by Marilyn Hacker

W. W. Norton & Company
New York · London

Copyright © 1986 by Marilyn Hacker
All rights reserved, including the
right of reproduction in whole or in
part in any form.

First published as a Norton paperback 1995

Manufacturing by The Haddon Craftsmen, Inc.

Library of Congress Cataloging-in-Publication Data

Hacker, Marilyn, 1942–
    Love, death, and the changing of the seasons.

    I. Title.
PS3558.A28L6   1986   811´.54   86-10776

ISBN 0-393-31225-9

W. W. Norton & Company, Inc.
500 Fifth Avenue, New York, N.Y. 10110
W. W. Norton & Company Ltd.
10 Coptic Street, London WC1A 1PU

Printed in the United States of America

    3 4 5 6 7 8 9 0

This book is also for
Julie Fay
and
Jacqueline Lapidus

The author wishes to thank
the National Endowment
for the Arts, the Ingram
Merrill Foundation, and
the Michael Karolyi
Memorial Foundation for
providing the time and
some of the space in which
this book was written.

Grateful acknowledgment is made to the editors of the following periodicals in which poems in this book have appeared: *Boulevard, Calyx, Conditions, Contact II, Cream City Review, Feminist Studies, Gazette, Manhattan Poetry Review, The Massachusetts Review, Mirage, Open Places, Pequod, River Styx, Shenandoah, Womantide, The Women's Review of Books,* and *Yellow Silk.*

That time of year thou mayst in me behold
When yellow leaves, or none, or few, do hang
Upon those boughs which shake against the cold,
Bare, ruined choirs where late the sweet birds sang.
In me thou seest the twilight of such day
As after sunset fadeth in the west,
Which by and by black night doth take away,
Death's second self that seals up all in rest.
In me thou seest the glowing of such fire
That on the ashes of his youth doth lie,
As the deathbed whereon it must expire,
Consumed with that which it was nourished by.
This thou perceivest, which makes thy love more strong,
To love that well which thou must leave ere long.

    —William Shakespeare: "Sonnet 73"

The paired butterflies are already yellow with August
Over the grass in the West garden;
They hurt me. I grow older.
If you are coming down through the narrows of the river
 Kiang,
Please let me know beforehand,
And I will come out to meet you
    As far as Cho-fu-Sa.

 —Ezra Pound: "The River-Merchant's Wife: A Letter"

I

Runaways Café I

You hailed a cab outside the nondescript
yuppie bar on Lexington to go
downtown. Hug; hug: this time I brushed my lips
just across yours, and fire down below
in February flared. O bless and curse
what's waking up no wiser than it was.
I will not go to bed with you because
I want to very much. If that's perverse,
there are, you'll guess, perversions I'd prefer:
fill the lacunae in: one; two; three; four . . .
I did, cab gone. While my late bus didn't come,
desire ticked over like a metronome.
For you, someone was waiting up at home.
For me, I might dare more if someone were.

Runaways Café II

For once, I hardly noticed what I ate
(salmon and broccoli and Saint-Véran).
My elbow twitched like jumping beans; sweat ran
into my shirtsleeves. Could I concentrate
on anything but your leg against mine
under the table? It was difficult,
but I impersonated an adult
looking at you, and knocking back the wine.
Now that we both want to know what we want,
now that we both want to know what we know,
it still behooves us to know what to do:
be circumspect, be generous, be brave,
be honest, be together, and behave.   *so funny!*
At least I didn't get white sauce down my front.

February 25

Dear Bill, I dawdled answering your letter.
My punishment—the postal rates were raised.
The mail piled on this table has me fazed.
I think of it as clearing up the clutter.
There's somebody I like better and better
—she's someone else's lover, though; not mine.
She hides her blushes in her leonine
hair, that was more like tinsel than like butter
when I ruffled it—the feminine   *uncle's affection*
of *avuncular*. She's twenty-five,   → *for a niece.*
but age is not the muddle of the matter
whose damp wings are unfolding now, alive
out of the chrysalis that I felt shatter   ✓
when I kissed her till heat split my spine.

Lesbian Ethics, or: Live Girl-Girl Sex Acts

It's not that I'm inimical to sleaze.
I most fondly remember getting it on
with her, crammed standing in an airplane john,
airsprayed, spotlit, jeans bunched around our knees,
or, in the Fiat, under some chestnut trees
in full view of the lunchbound *routiers,*
with *her.* Girl, I would have you any way
or where, except that infidelity's
the kind of bad taste that leaves a bad taste
worse than the mousebreath of a hangover.
I want you so much I can taste it, but
that's not the taste I want, though it means wast-
ing precocious spring waiting on hold, in rut,
for clean time to be your low-minded lover.

nice.

Lacoste I

Your being that age and my being this,
I wonder if you've spent some summer glad
to have not anything more than you had?
I did: through last July's parenthesis,
I worked, walked, ate, grew brown, wiry and lis-
some climbing paths along peach-orchards' plaid
on vineyards. But I'm bad at being bad,
and risk that satisfaction on a kiss,
over whose stile I'd beckon you beside
me to cull whitefleshed cherries from roadside
trees' yearly donation, compromise
the solitary moonwashed bed our eyes
would close exceeded in, where once I kept
my own counsel to soothe me while I slept.

Wagers

I bet you don't wear shoulder pads in bed.
I bet when we get over, we'll be *bad!*
I bet you blush all over when you come.

Although the butch coach gave them out, and said,
they're regulation issue for the team,
I bet you don't wear shoulder pads in bed;

and if I whispered something just unseem-
ly enough, I could make your ears turn red.
I bet you blush all over when you come

to where I say, I slept on what we did,
and didn't, then undressed you in a dream.
I bet you don't wear shoulder pads in bed.

I bet my blue pajamas split a seam
while I thought of my hand on you instead.
I bet you blush all over when you come.

Maybe I'll spend Bastille Day feeling bad,
deferring fireworks till the troops get home
—I bet you don't wear shoulder pads in bed.

Don't give me any; just promise me some.
I'm having nicer nightmares than I had.
I bet you blush all over when you come,

but I can bide my time until it's bid-
dable (though, damn, you make me squirm;
I bet you don't wear shoulder pads in bed),

wait till the strawberries are ripe for cream,
and get to give, for having kept my head.
I bet you blush all over when you come.
I bet you don't wear shoulder pads in bed.

O little one, this longing is the pits.
I'm horny as a timber wolf in heat.
Three times a night, I tangle up the sheet.
I seem to flirt with everything with tits:
Karyn at lunch, who knows I think she's cute;
my ex, the D.A. on the Sex Crimes Squad;
Iva's gnarled, canny New England god-
mother, who was my Saturday night date.
I'm trying to take things one at a time:
situps at bedtime, less coffee, less meat,
more showers, till a remedy appears.
Since there's already quite enough Sex Crime,
I think I ought to be kept off the street.
What are you doing for the next five years?

Well, damn, it's a relief to be a slut
after such lengths of "Man delights not me,
nor woman neither," that I honestly
wondered if I'd outgrown it. Chocolate
or wine, a cashmere scarf, a cigarette,
had more to do with sensuality
than what's between my belly and my butt
that yearns toward you now unabashedly.
I'd love to grip your head between my thighs
while yours tense toward your moment on my ears,
but I'll still be thankful for this surprise
if things turn out entirely otherwise,
and we're bar buddies who, in a few years,
will giggle about this after two beers.

Didn't Sappho say her guts clutched up like this?
Before a face suddenly numinous, *divine, spiritlike*
her eyes watered, knees melted. Did she lactate
again, milk brought down by a girl's kiss?
It's documented torrents are unloosed
by such events as recently produced
not the wish, but the need, to consume, in us,
one pint of Maalox, one of Kaopectate.
My eyes and groin are permanently swollen,
I'm alternatingly brilliant and witless
—and sleepless: bed is just a swamp to roll in.
Although I'd cream my jeans touching your breast,
sweetheart, it isn't lust; it's all the rest
of what I want with you that scares me shitless.

Though sometimes now we sound like fiancées
curmurring futures that augment like growths,
I've never touched you underneath your clothes,
or seen you more than twice in seven days.
I venture it's a trifle premature
to sign the china-pattern registry
before you are, at least, at liberty
to hang your PJ's on my bathroom door.
A funny pair of homebodies we are,
as wicked as we like to paint ourselves:
I kiss you till my clit's about to burst,
and catch myself reorganizing shelves.
Let's go to some disreputable bar
and do a little fancy dancing first.

Lacoste II

"I don't think you'd bulldoze my living room,"
you said. Well, hon, your bulldozer is flattening
my vineyard on the hillside, threatening
the goatherd's path through yellow stands of broom
I followed through subsiding afternoon
heat, picking my way as I picked out words
in counterpoint to the good news of birds'
crepuscular announcements, quite alone,
contentedly anticipating no
agape other than my evening meal,
its dialogue the book's beside my plate.
O leave your hard-hat on the driver's seat
and follow me down to the river. O
listen, Rachel, to the nightingale.

Lacoste III

Nate, the next-door neighbor, is a jazzman,
an eighty-year-old black expatriate,
as lean as his Australian Nancy's fat.
She's redolent of turpentine and jasmine
—she paints. Some nights, his homesick saxophone
—no, not homesick, exactly: retrospective—
incises New Orleans on the collective
winegrowers' banner sky, where a tired moon,
filed down to a guitarist's fingernail,
picks out a single semi between towns
in the broad, shallow valley I look down
on from the rooftop railing alongside.
We'll listen, late; wait morning in that wide
bed, downstairs. Or I'll wait, for the mail. nice.

International Women's Day, 1985

Mommy was fragile, and she stank of smoke.
Iva, with gerbil graveyards in her hair,
sprawled, puffy-faced, across the rose club chair,
like the punchline of a dead-baby joke,
though all *she'd* done was read till twelve in bed.
Mommy was nonetheless efficiency's
avatar: groomed her, hugged her, found her keys,
hoisted her knapsack onto her, and said,
"À tout à l'heure! Sois sage et travaille bien!"
and closed the door, and thought of you again,
wakeful, maybe, in your squash-court living room
I've seen once, in the sofa-bed you share
with someone, who, this morning, isn't there.
Hello, sweetheart, it's seven-twelve AM.

You, little one, are just the kind of boy
I would have eyeballed at the bar, and cruised
efficiently, and taken home, and—used?
Hell, no! The bodice-busters say "enjoy,"
and how I do enjoy what girl you bring
back out in me, brought out in time for you
to riff all keys of titillation through
with those square, reddish hands whose quivering
sometimes on mine plucks songs from everything.
Bad, brash, and skinless, not a boy at all,
between boot-tops and that surprising small
waist is where my hands and mouth would slide,
effortless and attentive to you, guide
you, ride you to the place we both belong.

Copines/Tapdancing

"Nadja," I said, *"ces gosses me font chier!*
The night before my party, one has *crises*
at home, *mine* oversleeps and breez-
es off to school without her lunch—today!"
So, in a taxi, in a traffic jam,
I messengered the sandwiches crosstown,
instead of pinning up the Empire gown
I'm resurrecting to declare "Hot damn!"
to all and sundry at tonight's event.
"It's an event; it isn't destiny.
Rappelle-toi de ça," Marie reminded me,
when I let on what impetus had sent
me diving for my notebook and my crotch
these days. Well, can I make it happen? Watch!

Hey, listen, the day when it's you and me
heart to cunt to heart to cunt, all clear
for me to call and say, "Get over here
now, girl!" and you would, with your own key,
let yourself in—and I would have one too,
for your door—then, I'll swear off, if it bugs
you, giving enthusiastic hugs
to my girlfriends, with *quelques gros bisous*
(at least, not on the lips, in front of you).
I don't sleep around. I sleep right here.
(These nights, I don't sleep too much anywhere.)
I can't say, "*When* you coming over?" yet.
Until we get at where we're going to,
I need as much hugging as I can get.

Iva's coppery, your rain-blonde, head,
one nuzzling into each unstalwart shoulder.
I stroke your neck with one hand, with one, hold her.
Nice work, if I can get it. Sure, she said
she knew what we were up to, when I told her,
thought it was cool, but thought she'd be discreet,
liked you a lot, and did she have to eat
the vegetables? This evening, I've installed her
at a school friend's for the night, and added,
don't come home in the morning before ten,
and felt that I was doing something bad. Did
I start to make this harder for her then?
Tonight, you will or won't get in my pants.
Tomorrow night, fair stands the wind for France.

First, I want to make you come in my hand
while I watch you and kiss you, and if you cry,
I'll drink your tears while, with my whole hand, I
hold your drenched loveliness contracting. And
after a breath, I want to make you full
again, and wet. I want to make you come
in my mouth like a storm. No tears now. The sum
of your parts is my whole most beautiful
chart of the constellations—your left breast
in my mouth again. You know you'll have to be
your age. As I lie beside you, cover me
like a gold cloud, hands everywhere, at last
inside me where I trust you, then your tongue
where I need you. I want you to make me come.

Fear of Flying

I won't go down in flames till I've gone down
on you. I won't go down anyway,
except in your brushfire. I would say, stay
with me tonight. I wouldn't say no. I've done
the peephole-watch where you stride off like Shane.
If I wake up at wolf-hour, cub, I want
to suck my fingers that taste of your cunt,
and gently infiltrate the tangled mane
around your sleepy face, and tug and stroke
and lick you just awake enough to start
over. But there's been enough wind-change warning
to counsel having a good line for part-
ing in separate cabs at midnight with a joke:
"Night, angel—call me later in the morning."

I almost lost it, but I got it back,
didn't I, in time: some parting repartée,
then wraparound "Just Walk Away, Renée,"
with my Amelia scarf and my knapsack,
out of the hallway into the wee hours?
You couldn't have been upstairs, yet, but in case
you were watching, I squared shoulders and face,
flourished a cab like conjurors pluck flowers
out of the air. You were so good; I messed
up while you were showing me your best
privacies. I was whisked off in the rain,
feeling your age, and counting out the rhymes.
What was that fine line of yours: "Sometimes
the only thing that moves me is a plane."

A couple' Jewish bitches singing Motown
with some pizzazz, in gender-bender shoes,
funky and late and smoky, almost lowdown
enough, since even white girls get the blues
sometimes, and have to sing something about it:
there's nothing else to do at half-past-five,
four miles apart, and getting by without it
—three thousand miles tonight. If I'm alive
as this because I'm lodged inside your spine,
you in my gut, my dirty-voiced young lover,
we'll do just fine when we can jam together
the necessary parts. We'll do just fine.
One more pre-dawn reprise of "Stormy Weather,"
until we get down, girl, when we get over.

Lacoste IV

It's almost as if we're already there,
in the narrow stone house, me upstairs
writing at the splintery pine table,
you in the downstairs study, with its cradle
of a marriage bed, slit window looking
into the Buniols' herb garden. I'm cooking
a sonnet sequence and a cassoulet
with goose from Carcassonne, let *mijoter*
on the burner till nightfall. The vow
of silence breaks at seven. It's noon now.
Pleasure delayed is pleasure amplified
—I'll show you these bitch Welsh quatrains I've tried.
It's your turn to work outdoors in the sun
on the roof—your footsteps, and the last line's done.

II

In-Flight Movies

Packed four abreast across a DC10
between a scented yuppie and a plugged-
in Iva (Cyndi Lauper is the drug),
I find a clean page to find you again,
shielding it with my elbow—why ashamed?
The flight time and the film have been announced
—about a drunken poet, and pronounced,
in French, like someone saying, twice, your name.
Speaking of drunken poets, here's the wine
—white Burgundy. You'd say it was all right.
I'm tired and crowded, but my appetite's
there. Iva, all elbows, sings out of tune.
I'm feeling claustrophobic, and resigned
I won't make the Five Mile High Club tonight.

vowel rhyme here.
very nice

Jeunesse Coiffure

Here's where we are: Iva's being shampooed,
and I have just been sheared like a bad boy.
(She cropped me in October, too.) The joy
of being back in the *quartier*'s imbued,
this morning, with a certain *douce-amère*.
Iva gets corn-rows. I riffle *Le Monde*.
Creme rinse ad: *gamine* brunette, head on blonde
friend's shoulder . . . Cool it. You will like this hair-
cut—it gives me, well, an attitude.
I'll tug your flip, and . . . Never mind. I'm where
I know my way around, in the Marais,
ten paces from the Grandes Marques Dégriffées,
since Iva hasn't got a thing to wear.
I think the women in the ad are nude.

Grand Hotel Malher

Iva woke me up by rolling on me,
coughing and mumbling. Bitch, I knew you'd laugh.
I prodded her back to the other half
of the bed, but now I'm sitting on the john. We
ate at the Basque local, "Le Fandango."
Jackie and I had *magret de canard,*
and split a Mercurey *(rouge)* to our hard
times, while Iva devoured *escargots.*
We'd hit the shops. All three of us did dress
the part. (Why shouldn't girls *parler chiffons?*)
Now I've got huge cotton pajamas on.
My watch still says eleven-thirty. Guess
what time that is here. *Le chien suit le loup;*
can't even let my hand stand in for you.

Poète Maudite

Umbrellas outside the Samaritaine
go up against unseasonable snow.
You are, at least, too old to be Rimbaud,
and I'm too hardheaded to be Verlaine.
Slant light on sleet: I walk across the Seine
toward Annie's gallery, rue Bonaparte.
There are lines of yours I know by heart.
There are scents of yours soaked in my skin.
Just as I dragged my bags into the hall,
a six-foot-four Jamaican Heurtebise
brought me your sonnets, and took mine away.
(Depopulating the Quai Malaquais,
I can imagine you down on your knees,
your mouth on me in the sunsplashed snowfall.)

Le Manuscrit

Four women in a restaurant for gay men,
feasting, after Marthe and I had seen
a play, while Iva watched Jax' miniscreen:
Iva, mouth full: "Mom, Ray is *seventeen*
years younger than you are?" I snort, the others
snicker. It was "birthdays" brought it on.
"Marie is how much older?"
                              "Twenty-one
years. No problems."
                        "Yeah, but you're *friends,* not lovers."
I could say to you both, my casuists,
that we've not yet been tempered by the fire
scorching our skivvies, and that makes us—what?
Two thousand years of Western literature:
potions and swords, the quests, the songs, the trysts,
call us what Iva, if she knew, would not.

Meanwhile

Sunday, Monday—you're back in your real life,
now, housesitting an Upper East Side flat,
likely in bed—I don't think about that—
with her, whom you, not kidding, call "my wife."
You still live with someone you still love.
I know it, though it isn't what I want
to know. I've put my "older confidante"
hat on, listened, and said, often enough:
"If she is, she will be 'family'."
(David rang up today; Joanna wrote.)
"You need a door that closes." (So do I.)
Have I added, have you had to infer
the truth that's always catching in my throat,
"I'm still here for you if you stay with her"?

What You Might Answer

"I'm going to do what *I* want just this once!
Plums dropped in laps are often overripe.
I don't eat liver, and I won't eat tripe.
Nobody needs her Frye boots cast in bronze.
I don't like crowds, and now I'm feeling crowded.
I can speak tongues, but not the ones your friends
gossip with you about me in. The end's
still moot, jackboots. I have to think about it.
Two yards of hair, two miles of legs—and she
is also who's, for years, seen what I've seen.
We both need to be twenty-five years old.
You want a masturbation fantasy?
Some girls you know put out a magazine
full of them—but I'm not the centerfold."

Which didn't deter me then from lying down
on Jackie's couch, for the first time in days,
to let my hands and mind go back a ways,
and forward, in, against, above, around,
until I said your name (what corn) and came.
(I didn't muck up the upholstery,
Jax.) (Iva took a break from me
to read in the hotel room.) It's a game,
it's hot flashes, it's "Roxanne's Revenge,"
it's Mother Superior on a binge
with laughing gas inflating her bad habit.
(If you eat pussy, why won't you eat rabbit?)
It's what in this bright world I would like best:
your mind on my mind; your breasts on my breasts.

Rue du Pont Louis-Philippe

Iva said, "Wouldn't it be neat if we
got a place here, *trois chambres, cuisine, salon,*
and if Nadja just sort of gave up on
Lacoste, and sold us the house in the country?
We'd live here in the winter, and weekends
and summers in Lacoste!"

                         "I'd kidnap Ray,"
I tweaked her, as we elbowed passageway
through lunchtime schoolkids.

                           "And *then* my best friend's
mother put her *en pension* here, and she
could spend weekends with us—and then all four
of us, you and Ray and me and Mandy,
got a big car! Mom, how come things never are
as good as I could make them up to be?"
"There's still ice cream on the Île Saint-Louis!"

Le Départ

I would get up and fling myself on Paris,
walking to Montparnasse from the Marais
before ten in the morning of the day
I'd leave, eyes streaming in the wind, embarrass-
ing self and shopkeepers with such excess
feeling. We leave tonight. But now I head
for any table (Iva's still in bed)
and open up my permanent address,
the cardboard covers between which I live
with you. I'm sleeping better. I don't dream
about you, but I always wake up with
you, bathe with you, zip up, go downstairs
for (you'd have tea) my coffee without cream,
seeing this blonde light in your morning hair.

En Train I

Here's what I made up to amuse myself:
we might cross the Alps in a *wagon-lit,*
plunge in each other as we mount from sea-
level, till, from the narrow web-strapped shelf
two altos *a cappella* chime the glass,
beyond which: snowpeaks, black sky, stars, stars, stars.
My snoring seatmate in the smoking car
bumps me on one side. Iva has an ass
like a tool box. Railmen on strike again
cancelled our train. On one with no *couchettes*
vacant, we've *places assises* we rushed to get,
next to a Genoese mamma in black
who won the one spare seat for her trick back.
So much for sonnets about sex on trains.

En Train II

And right there in the middle of the night,
sleeping with strangers on a train, I doubted
you, and myself. How could I have allowed it,
me, to go this far, aimed to end in spite
of us in bitterness, blankness, unnec-
essary pain. I couldn't see your face.
I couldn't see us together anyplace.
I thought of wanting more and having less
than before, diminished by desire
gone needy, weedy, and gone out too deep
to go home (when the world used to be home).
Then, like a rescue copter lit by crossfire,
I saw your face across that daft schoolroom
from me. I smiled—grinned, really—and went to sleep.

Primavera

O my harbinger of the equinox,
your season drenches me in Florentine
rain. The Arno and the streets are green.
Iva helped Liana fix a box
from the greengrocer's for the pregnant cat
who's due to drop a litter any minute.
They put wood shavings and torn papers in it,
and hid it in a corner of the flat
(two stories, *quattrocento*) where she might
hunt it out and claim it for her own.
Perched on an antique escritoire, the phone
doesn't stop ringing—friends of friends who bring
seasons of messages. Yours was the spring:
lie down with me before Midsummer Night.

Substitute Teacher

Midnight here; six there: you face Marie
and the others at the seminar
table. She stares you down a bit. You've bar-
gained to be third to read. Before that, she
has everyone, her too, writing *sur place*
on "place," as in "Florence," or "Your place or mine?"
She's so damn good I think I should resign.
I know that every woman in the class
will at least fantasize a *tête-à-tête*
with her, after, sure that her mind's met
theirs already. I am selfish, but,
I hope you two, together in some bar,
talk about us, and poetry, before
my dawn's your midnight, and your door is shut.

nice.

Shopping

Iva said, "I could see Rachel in that hat.
It looks kind of—official—but in fun
colors." Between Fedora and Stetson . . .
She might be right. But then, what size? I'd caught
myself, earlier, looking at a ring:
gold, a square garnet. Absolutely not!
That says too much, though we have said a lot.
Bijoux in sock drawers are embarrassing,
and one ring finger is already dressed.
Silk ties are safe. Do you like model cars
as much as I do? No briefcases, or leather
accoutrements for San Francisco bars.
Bars, here, mean coffee, and we need a rest.
I wish we three were being girls together.

Il Cibrēo

White tablecloths in front, for fêting raises
or anniversaries. Go in the back
door, though (marked *Vini e Olli,* round the block
in one of those unmarked alleys like mazes),
and there's a room behind the kitchen: wooden
tables, straw placemats, anemones in jugs.
Students in dufflecoats meet here, with hugs
and backchat. The young waiter plunked a good and
toothy unlabeled red down for a start.
Iva, who opts for Life in lieu of Art
and looked on Petrarch (frescoed, twice life-size
in the Uffizi) plain, looked in my eyes
with round-cheeked candor, and said what she thinks
we *do,* offhand. No wonder Mommy drinks!

After the Telegram

My eyelids fly open like windowshades
minutes before the birds, before the bells.
My hand is on my own right breast, which swells
to the month, to the touch. (Getting laid's
not on my mind, but is it under my skin!)
My innards are reminding me of last
night's meal, when—yes, it did happen, that fast:
a note taped to my door; your voice on the phone;
me rolling with my wine on the parquet;
Julie, still rumpled off the train from Rome,
sure she'd walked into an eighteenth-century
madhouse. From behind a sliding door,
Liana's voice drew Iva's, reassur-
ing her she'd still find her own home, at home. || *poor Iva.*

Instamatic

Julie and I are sitting on the grass
in the sun, in front of a cathedral
closed for lunch. Beneath a tetrahedral
obelisk, young Europeans pass
postprandial booze, barefoot, *bandes dessinées*
in hand. *She* has my poems in hand, and yours.
As the basilica opens its doors,
the kids pack up their wine and file away.
"You guys are crazy, but it's great," she said.
(We've put up with each other through a lot
of moods, mileage, and meals; we've swapped and read
first drafts where no one for kilometers
reads English—so I am itching to know what
hot crit's cooked now behind that frown of hers.)

a single sonnet
can go only
so deep:
Hacker triumps by
ending @ the beginning
of a new idea as much
or more than when she ties it
all together @ the end.

March Wind

I almost came in my new herringbones
in the Via degli Alfani, just
imagining your *socks* off. Wind, you must
blow me back to my own one, though the stones
of Florence glisten in late-March sunshine.
If I were here a month, and home tomorrow,
with you tonight, but with a week to borrow
between shops' reopening and bedtime
(if you, O if you, if you O were here),
I wouldn't abridge this season by an hour.
I taste the morning light with such desire
as I will (say I will) take from the flower
of you, touch as I will learn your entire
country, these tender hills seen from a tower.

Mythology

Penelope as a *garçon manqué*
weaves sonnets on a barstool among sailors,
tapping her iambs out on the brass rail. Ours
is not the high-school text. Persephone
a.k.a. Télémaque-who-tagged-along,
sleeps off her lunch on an Italian train
headed for Paris, while Ulysse-Maman
plugs into the Shirelles singing her song
("What Does a Girl Do?"). What *does* a girl do
but walk across the world, her kid in tow,
stopping at stations on the way, with friends
to tie her to the mast when she gets too
close to the edge? And when the voyage ends,
what does a girl do? Girl, that's up to you.

La Sirène

You're a good disc jockey, you know that?
I let myself long for you with the ear-
phones on, watching Tuscany disappear.
Simon & Garfunkel weren't half bad,
though the guitarist whom I listened to
was you, pouring all those extravagant
declarations in my ears. You meant
me to, mind-bender, even before you knew
what you could sing me back to. Getting wet
inside, I stood out in the corridor
with a teenaged Italian space cadet
tuned into his own message-on-cassette,
indulging what felt like nostalgia for
all kinds of things that haven't happened yet.

Future Conditional

After the supper dishes, let us start
where we left off, my knees between your knees,
half in the window seat. O let me, please,
hands in your hair, drink in your mouth. Sweetheart,
your body is a text I need the art
to be constructed by. I halfway kneel
to your lap, propped by your thighs, and feel
burning my hand, your privacy, your part
armor underwear. This time I'll loose
each button from its hole; I'll find the hook,
release promised abundance to this want,
while your hands, please, here and here, exigent
and certain, open this; it is, this book,
made for your hands to read, your mouth to use.

Les Carabosses

Il y avait au moins une trentaine de gouines
(that's "dykes" in French) come to listen to me
sound off (in French) and read some poetry
(in English). Not averse to being seen
as an amelioration of the view,
I wore that black nubbed-raw-silk *salopette,*
—but with a lurex cowlneck under it;
the neckline-to-the-waist take was for you.
Spiffed in silk tweed (with shoulder pads), Jax took
pictures, beamed back when I read translations
she'd made last week from my old and my new book,
and, since I've undertaken that career
too, I could say, to close (approximation):
"This is by Rachel, whom I wish were here."

*Rachel gets
a nice career
boost from an aging(?)
affluent dyke. Yikes.*

Rive Droite

The sky is melancholy and severe.
The *quartier juif*, after a week of rain,
goes gray on gray on gray, Nullepart-sur-Seine.
I make phonecalls *à n'en jamais finir*.
I have to see at least six people here
before the *bateau ivre* embarks again.
Hilarity last night with Argentine
lovers-in-exile: three polyglot queer
women and one pre-polyglot pre-
pubescent, who is writing fantasy
fiction crosslegged in a barrel chair
now, across Jax' living room from me.
Our flight is later than I'd like. Be there.
Bring your briefcase and some clean underwear.

Symbiose

Across the bridge and up the rue Saint-Jacques,
Iva mugged and flirted like a mad thing.
"Oui, je déconne, je suis complètement dingue!"
she shouted, flinging her arm across my back.
Hung across my neck, forty-six kilos
glued a long wet one to my cheek, a short
dry one to my lips, then, *"Tu es morte!*
Piff! Pow!"* From a billboard for Dunlopillos,
"Voulez-vous coucher avec moi?" she read.
"Désolée, mais franchement pas!"
                              *"Voulez-vous
coucher avec Rachel?"*

                    "Je mentirais pas, oui,"
at which both of us giggled wickedly,
and I kissed the top of her unwashed head,
not at all certain what she's going through.

The Dark Night of the 747   I

We're somewhere—I don't know precisely where.
We leave tonight; we nested yesterday,
acquired for Iva an elephant-gray
lit-pliant for our promised *pied-à-terre*
three flights up in the rue de Turenne.
I ate too much. My head hurts. I feel sick.
I want these twenty hours over quick-
ly, the ocean crossed, New York again
under foot. I want to be with you. O
departure's inevitably limbo,
mind gone ahead, body behind. *Quand même,*
I'm going to see a flat in the *deuxième*
that might be buyable. Let this white night
approaching end in my bed, with you, all right?

The Dark Night of the 747   II

Hope is a forked and not a feathered thing.
I didn't suffer going; coming back,
my neck aches, my temples throb with thumbtacked
reminders, a scratched chalkboard's shivering
into my ribs. Guess what—I'm terrified.
Will we get there? We're late—will you be still
around? Will this be a *poisson d'avril?*
I can't envision what will happen, tried
and stymied myself nightly. That's not true,
exactly. I've spent years of nights with you
in ten, come in your honor if not in
your arms. But what will be our dailiness?
That's where I censor my imagination.
I don't think I've a right to it, I guess.

The Dark Night of the 747   III

This crown of thorns is just a *gueule de bois.*
Jax says, we go so often that for us
hopping the ocean's like catching a bus.
Serai-je en six heures à côté de toi?
Were this gent's elbows just a foot away,
I could lean back and think of you, escape
in fantasy like Iva with her tape
playing—but he's in half my seat. *Allez,
Monsieur!* Sweetheart, half Paris dykedom knows
I'm flying west, my courage in my toes,
all trepidations like a picture bride.
This guy's expansive wingspan would unhinge
a Buddhist nun. Hey, Iva, let's switch sides!
On crowded flights, even commuters cringe.

The Dark Night of the 747   IV

My life is waiting just beyond the *douane*
maybe, while I'm waiting for valises
to roll out of the rain. This story teases
unmercifully. I guess it's in the plan.
Well, I'm in one piece, both feet on the ground,
intestines churning with anticipation.
Who'd wait for me past midnight? Are you patient?
The same wet suitcases trolley around.
I've always been stoic toward such delays
—lunch hour for luggage handlers, one's bags last
inevitably. I've put off for days
waiting to wait. I want to get out fast
and find you out there, if out there you are,
star of my long night, with a rented car.

III

In her own room, all through that doubled length
of night, Iva kept on her traveling
clothes, and the lights. While we did everything
two punchdrunk girls on second wind, whose strength
was tenfold, because, hey, our hearts were pure-
ly bent on it, could, she, her native clutter
of toys around her, kept watch (door closed, but her
transom showed the light). I'm still not sure
of what she made of what she thought she heard.
Six-thirty, and I went from you to her.
She'd put on her pit-stop mechanic suit. *beautiful.*
"Things are going to be different than they were,
Squodge," I said to my daughter the diplomat,
"but I love you, you know, down to my last, best word."

The calendar turned over: two days later
she'd gone. ("Just Walk Away, Renée," and "Shane"
relevant here.) *"Sois sage et travaille bien,"*
lunch bag, book bag into the elevator.
Four weeks before she'll kick the door again;
four weeks to be loose girls with one another.
It's part-time strange to be a part-time mother.
("Persephone, dear, don't speak to strange men,"
and so forth.) You should know, there's times I've cried
when she called to say she'd come back a day
later. One night I had a family
—my two girls messing with the French typewriter.
I could stay in the kitchen now to write, or
get back under the covers by your side.

Cabbing it south to my first night at your
place in the rain, I had a *déjà vu*.
I hadn't copied what I'd made for you
the last few days. When it happened before
(but it hadn't), you were pissed. I'm easy,
says the song. An ambulance, alarm
pulsing, weaves the Drive. Now, the flash storm
stopped, wet streets shine. You worry how to please me.
(I'll tell you ways and ways again at leisure.)
The sidewalk's empty in your part of town.
Three flights of stairs lead to the deck you cleared
another stormy night (I'm hot; I'm scared)
where you may not be thinking about pleasure.
Sometimes, after the rain, the lines are down. ✓

Note to Elaine the speech pathologist:
grief tumbles into lust, a crush can cruise
across some conversations to, good news,
a choice, and ladies who have gone unkissed
beyond a certain age can get a chance
to demonstrate they've not forgotten how
to do it. I am fully forty-two
—there was no disco when I learned to dance—
but there's some girl left in the old life yet.
I think you've noticed that I'm getting some
brand-old ideas (fifty-seven poems
in seven weeks, Elaine!) and I *can* kiss
ennui goodbye. Just for the record, this
girl got as much girl as she hoped to get.

Eight Days in April

[handwritten: half-a-crown 7 poems.]

1. I broke a glass, got bloodstains on the sheet: *[a]*
    hereafter, must I only write you chaste *[b]*
    connubial poems? Now that I have traced *[b]*
    a way from there to here across the sweet- *[a]*
    est morning, rose-blushed blonde, will measured feet *[a]*
    advance processionally, where before *[c]*
    they (scuff-heeled) flights of stairs, kicked at a door, *[c]* *[handwritten: (verb)]*
    or danced in wing-tips to a dirty beat? *[a]*
    Or do I tell the world that I have got *[a]*
    rich quick, got lucky (got laid), got just what *[a]*
    the doctor ordered, more than I deserved? *[d]*
    This is the second morning I woke curved *[d]*
    around your dreaming. In one night, I've seen *[e]*
    moonset and sunrise in your lion's mane. *[e]*

2. Moons set and suns rise in your lion's mane *a*
through LP kisses or spread on my thighs. *b*
Winter subsided while I fantasized *b*
what April dawns frame in the windowpane. *a*
Sweetheart, I'm still not getting enough sleep, *c*
but I'm not tired, and outside it's spring *d*
in which we sprang the afternoon shopping *d*
after I'd been inside you, O so deep *c*
I thought we would be tangled at the roots. *e*
I think we are. (I've never made such noise. *f*
I've never come so hard, or come so far *g*
in such a short time.) You're an exemplar *g*
piss-elegance is not reserved for boys. *f*
Tonight we'll go out in our gangster suits. *e*

3. Last night we went out in our gangster suits,
   but just across the street to Santerello's,
   waited past nine for wine. We shone; the fellows
   noticed. "You have a splendid linen coat,"
   Dimitri told you as he sat us down.
   (This used to be my local; now it's chic.)
   A restaurant table's like a bed: we speak
   the way we do calmed after love, alone
   in the dark. There's a lot to get to know.
   We felt bad; we felt better. Soon I was
   laid back enough to drink around the bend.
   You got me home, to bed, like an old friend.
   I like you, Rachel, when you're scared, because
   you tough it out while you're feeling it through.

the name.
what happened
to Rachel? ?
who is she.
is she still
writing

4.   You tough it out while you're feeling it through:
sometimes the bed's rocked over tidal waves
that aren't our pleasures. Everyone behaves
a little strangely when they're in a new
neighborhood, language, continent, time zone.
We got here fast; your jet lag's worse than mine.
I only had Paris to leave behind.
You left your whole young history. My own
reminds me to remind you, waking shaken
with tears, dream-racked, is standard for the course.
We need accommodation that allows
each one some storage space for her dead horse.
If the title weren't already taken,
I'd call this poem "Directions to My House."

5. I'd call this poem "Directions to My House," *a*
    except today I'm writing it in yours, *b*
    in your paisley PJ's. The skylight pours *b*
    pale sunlight on white blankets. While I douse *a*
    my brain with coffee, you sleep on. Dream well *c*
    this time. We'll have three sets of keys apiece: *d*
    uptown, downtown, Paris on a sublease. *d*
    Teach me to drive. (Could I teach you to spell?) *c*
    I think the world's our house. I think I built *e*
    and furnished mine with space for you to move *f*
    through it, with me, alone in rooms, in love *f*
    with our work. I moved into one mansion *g*
    the morning when I touched, I saw, I felt *e*
    your face blazing above me like a sun. *g*

6. Your face blazing above me like a sun-
    deity, framed in red-gold flames, *gynandre*
    in the travail of pleasure, urgent, tender
    terrible—my epithalamion
    circles that luminous intaglio
    —and you under me as I take you there,
    and you opening me in your mouth where
    the waves inevitably overflow
    restraint. No, no, that isn't the whole thing
    (also you drive like cop shows, and you sing
    gravel and gold, are street-smart, book-smart,
    laugh from your gut) but it is (a soothing
    poultice applied to my afflicted part)
    the central nervous system and the heart.

7.   The central nervous system and the heart,
     and whatever it is in me wakes me
     at 5 AM regardless, and what takes me
     (when you do) ineluctably apart
     and puts me back together; the too-smart,
     too-clumsy kid glutted on chocolate cakes (me
     at ten); the left-brain righteousness that makes me
     make of our doubled dailiness an art
     are in your capable square hands. O sweet,
     possessives make me antsy: we are free
     to choose each other perpetually.
     Though I don't think my French short-back-and-sides
     means I'll be the most orthodox of brides,
     I broke a glass, got bloodstains on the sheet.

On Marriage

Epithalamion? Not too long back
I was being ironic about "wives."
It's very well to say, creation thrives
on contradiction, but that's a fast track
shifted precipitately into. Tack-
y, some might say, and look mildly appalled. On
the whole, it's one I'm likely to be called on.
Explain yourself or face the music, Hack.
No law books frame terms of this covenant.
It's choice that's asymptotic to a goal,
which means that we must choose, and choose, and choose
momently, daily. This moment my whole
trajectory's toward you, and it's not los-
ing momentum. Call it anything we want.

After eight nights of sleeping with you, one
without you, and, O damn it, I miss you.
I'd have to say how much and where I'd kiss you
into your answering machine. It's on;
you're out. I'd like to brag that I have done
my donkey work, cleared my desk. In a daze,
I walked four miles enumerating ways
you make me laugh, take care of business, moan
your name out loud and . . . There's the telephone!
Midnight, your good friend/roommate's sick, maybe, gone
off without telling you. I saw Chip and Iva.
You got in trouble in your sailor bar.
I drank wine, talked France, and you, with Nadja.
We wish we were together. Well, we are.

Saturday Morning

While you sleep off the brandy, little one,
my hand could find its way back to the place
it knows so well, now. Even with your face
turned away from me, sleeping in till noon,
you move right through me. After we were done
talking (thence the brandy) until four
AM, you, in the dark, played three songs for
me while I dozed—so tired I couldn't come
when you'd tried for me. So you sat on the floor
with the guitar, beside me, troubador,
and then, naked, you woke me to you, brought me
down on your mouth, brought it down and caught me
in the gray dawn, whose sunburst was your name
like brandy in my mouth as I came and came.

Saturday Night

Drunk, in the island dark, up a rope ladder
onto a ferry deck, one night, you climbed.
We're feeling our way down one now, to I'm
not sure what ground, what depth. Happier, sadder
than ever, in one hour, over a meal
(retsina, moussaka, broiled shrimp) we go
into each other's histories, don't know
whether the next rung's bottom. How to deal
with the beat-up Mercedes' unkempt driver
waiting for your Cessna to arrive, or
to get out of that swamp where I'd bred snakes
those last two years, fast—blind night landing takes
some fancy footwork, strong hands. Fog's around
us, but we hold each other, on hard ground.

Sunday Night

"Sometimes you've got to let the kid win!"
Win what, from whom? You, in that book-lined room,
in a softball cap, with your looseleaf, are almost home
free, if you can get those last two lines in,
while I sweat an enjambment in the kitchen
—hearth of my house, now my heart's at its center.
Typewriters clatter. Trained for years, I enter
with some advantage in this competition.
Have we got Spartan lovers in the story? As
you may recall, "Beneath it, or upon it!"
Clangor of battle, stripling helot dies
to save his darling, smiling since his eyes
are on him. You swagger, victorious,
out to claim a drink, with another sonnet.

Monday, Monday

I wish Kim hadn't made a pass at you.
I wish she hadn't asked you not to tell me
she had. O hell, I wish that she would call me,
so she and I, *copines,* could talk it through.
She wants to call you when I'm not around.
Is white wine proper for a summit meeting?
. . . she called on my third glass, while I was eating
ham and cress, from a phonebooth in P'town.
After gossip: jobs, Mary Oliver,
and Jax *dépaysée,* it was easier
to say, "What *was* all that? It felt shitty!"
till we were working back to where we were
copines. As we wound down, the bell, the key
in the lock, *inattendu,* quicksilver.

Monday, Monday II

In the lock, *inattendu,* quicksilver
click, and you swaggered like gangbusters
in, so the phonecall about trust was
cut off. (It was long.) We were still ver-
balizing away while you typed what I'd
read when you left, and you would leave, it said.
A kiss, after seven phonecalls, to put me to bed.
A dozen more then, on the couch. The F.B.I.'d
got in the act. I don't launder money;
I don't do windows, I don't think I got
the point, though one or two points did get hot
in the process. You were as slow as honey
leaving a teaspoon, swirled into the cream.
I had one bad moment, and one bad dream.

Monday, Monday III

I had one bad moment, and one bad dream.
Asleep, I stretched my arm, assumed I'd touch
you; you weren't there; woke up: it wasn't much.
And then I got the soaps' scriptwriting team:
you had a girlfriend who lived out of town
who'd come to be with you the next few days,
and you asked if the two of you could stay
in Iva's room. and did. I got a phone-
call from Olga (Olga?) and recounted
this (dreaming) and she told me I was nuts,
while you and this redhead, in BVDs,
leaned in the door to say goodnight to me.
Good morning, ashtray full of Gauloises butts;
hello, New Jersey, with the fog around it.

. . . and Tuesday

Hello, New Jersey, with the fog around it;
hello coiled brown plastic umbilicus.
(AT&T and Yellow Cab keep us
in business; we, them.) I was not astounded
after you left, after the midnight call,
that this morning's weather bulletin
from Chelsea was: uncertain skies again.
Baby, the rain must, April rain must fall
—and I would just as soon stay home and wait
the storm out, wait for you to get to me
your way. Somehow I muster the aplomb
to say, if uptown feels like home, come home
tonight: there's food, there's wine, you've got the key.
I may go out. I won't be back that late.

and Tuesday II

I did go out. I didn't get back till late
morning the next day. Dinner out with Iva
(senior), who's much likelier to thrive, or
forget her aches, at least, if there's an eight
o'clock table laid with food and talk.
I brought Florentine snapshots, let her take
to keep one of her burgeoning namesake.
Most of the wine went my way, so I walked
her home, then on down West End Avenue,
the April wind filling my coat (a sail
on the drunken boat). I stopped to hail
a cab at Eighty-Sixth Street. Light after light
billowed it down the current of the night
toward what was, after all, our rendezvous.

and Tuesday III

Toward what was after, all our rendezvous
turned, fine-tuned as a classic Howard Hawkes:
the silken lady in the black suit walks
through the hotel bar, smoking. Point of view
hers: battered tweed with something on the rocks
near empty, quipping with the bartender,
glimpsed between bulky shoulders. Pan, then: send her
around the tables, till the eye-hook shocks:
"Hi, babe, have you been waiting for me long?"
Walking west on Twenty-Second Street,
in wind, near midnight (earlier Godard)
you held my coat closed, blocked gusts like a strong
and silent type; the dénouement inferred
upstairs: denim and silk pooled at our feet.

Bloomingdale's I

"If I weren't working, I'd sleep next to you
an hour or two more. Then we'd get the car
and drive a while, out of Manhattan, to
a quiet Bloomingdale's in Westchester.
If we saw anything we liked, we'd buy it!
We'd try things on, first, in one cubicle.
You'd need to make an effort to be quiet
when I knelt down and got my fingers full
of you, my mouth on you, against the wall.
You'd pull my hair. You'd have to bite your tongue.
I'd hold your ass so that you wouldn't fall.
Later, we'd take a peaceful walk along
the aisles, letting our hands touch every chance
they got, among the bras and underpants."

Bloomingdale's II

You are in conference in the epicure
section of Bloomingdale's, *ô ma délice*.
(If they knew what pomade your golden fleece
had had this morning, they'd singe it for sure.)
I've put on my hoodiest WilliWear
to lurk in by the English whole-grain mustard.
If I could catch your eye, you wouldn't be flustered.
We're going to take a shopping break downstairs
as soon as you can extricate yourself.
I'm getting tired of leaning on this shelf
and playing Spy; it's nonetheless a gas
to watch you being all efficiency.
Just now, you brush my shoulder as you pass.
"Hacker, follow me down to Lingerie!"

Bloomingdale's III

But Alice followed you to Lingerie
too, and upstairs. I didn't, but did know,
because you didn't jump me in the Girbaud
dressing room (one of my top ten fantasy
sites while we waited) or (even) stop for a long
kiss. We haven't talked much about those
years, yet, but sometimes the scenarios
must mirror. So we both tried things on
like Bronxville girls with their first credit cards.
I'm not half bad at picking out your clothes.
Your wardrobe was depleted by divorce,
but no, you're not diminished by shadows.
They're your sincerity. The part that's hard's
the part that lets me know we'll go the course.

Sweetheart, all day I've been listless and lame
after an evening so exceptionally
high. Class night: osmotic energy
got all the girls in gear. Tight forms to tame
only made them write funkier, slang
their diction down. I know some of them know
(besides Elaine); still, it was brash to throw
my Bic at you, and, oh dear, yes, I sang
"You Are My Soul and My Heart's Inspiration,"
to amplify the echoes in your poem.
Our cab-pool would have known that you came home
with me, but we stopped at The Balcony,
which has become our uptown filling station,
to wait for Kim and down a glass or three.

Kim rushed in, manic, twenty minutes late
after the six hours' drive from Provincetown.
We were already half-a-bottle down,
waiting for her, but she had had to wait
months for tomorrow's transatlantic flight
bringing her Danish lover from Stockholm.
She reminisced: the car we drove from Rome
through Tuscany, singing Supremes hits, till night
skies spoke French. A second bottle here
and now: the three of us were singing, too,
down Broadway, upstairs, a girl group; danced
all three, she and I, you and she. Her tears
caught her short; she disappeared, with you,
in the dark john. What's choice; what's circumstance?

Denim and silk pooled at our feet upstairs
in the hotel room. Everybody wore a
hot outfit for the weekend's diaspora.
. . . I called it that, and you assented. There's
cold heat in love that exiles make. Despair's
under the glistening surfaces. Who cried
after she came; who came after she cried?
Streetlights went off, then on again outside.
The landless lovers hit the tiles in pairs.
The icons of our ceremony are
glasses smashed underfoot in a gay bar
whose shards are swept out with the morning's trash.
"Where do the black girls dance?" Why do the Jews
go in for telegrams and wads of cash
close to the thigh? Our home is in the car
today. Baby, our home is in our shoes.

Sweet Things on Lex   *what is it?*

The East Side is, *comme on dirait,* intense.
With morning-after legs that may not serve, is
it any wonder that it makes me nervous
to sit with all these white people at once,
giving their complexes a Saturday
outing, so upward mobile I could shit?
My synapses are wired to opposite
walls of the room. It's me who's *dépaysée;*
two other lovers in my problematic
apartment. Drugs are one thing I shouldn't do.
We spent three hours this morning "caught in static";
you're having a restorative shampoo
around the corner. When I was sixteen
and split downtown, my gills felt just this green.

Dear Julie, Ray and I, in Central Park,
are sitting on my coat (like you and I
did, Florentine lunchtime), poetry
notebooks (ditto) in hand. She peeled the bark
off a sycamore twig (when it was stripped
it was the wheaten color of her hair)
as we talked, talked, talked. It seems that for
three weeks the conversation hasn't stopped,
except for love, so much, such thorough love
we're not presentable, though we've been going
out. She bought Iva a softball glove
and one for her, a first for each. They'll play
some rounds of catch out here (I hope) in May.
Right now it's April, and it isn't snowing.

I've taken refuge in Au Petit Beurre,
dawdling with an indifferent cappucino
after an early Zabar's run. I'll see now
what caffeine wit can be mustered before
going upstairs and being housemother
to Kim and Britt—who just bounced in and out
of here. I gave them *pains au chocolat*
and sent them off. This morning they're together;
we're not. I slept alone. Being alone
feels like old clothes, but I'm not sociable.
Somehow it's summer in New York in April.
Maybe five nights, or nine, or twenty-one will
get us together through the panic tunnel.
I'll have to listen better, little one.

Today's my turn outside the Customs pen,
waiting for Érzsi (whom I'd like to be
when I grow up), who telegrammed me
from Budapest: Arrive 15:15;
leave 18:30 for Chicago. Spend
three hours with her, in transit? *Pourquoi pas?*
So I have come as far as Cho-fu-Sa
for a refueling pit stop with my friend
the hero. Into damp air you could wade in
straggle baffled mid-European Jews
(comme nous, ma gosse), frock-coated, wigged, bag-laden;
some business polyglots, rucksacks, thick necks.
(All Jews, for all I know.) Hope she expects
this one turned courier, and brings the booze.

Symbiose II

We never begin drinking before seven.
We almost always have good appetites.
We always have good sex on Tuesday nights.
We like to give as good as we are given.
We like to do it in the morning; do
it also evenings between six and eight-
thirty. We like to have our dinner late.
We try to keep the body count to two
dead soldiers: this with moderate success.
We do get headaches, but we don't get cramps.
We take less than a half an hour to dress;
need: pockets, details, stuffs that please the touch.
We do it once like ladies, once like tramps.
We love each other very very much.

I don't want to push papers one more minute
or ever pack another fourth-class parcel!
My nerves are giddy players in a farce—well,
I guess that this is love, and that I'm in it,
but how I'm longing for the long days messing
with breakfast dishes, or with *bricolage,*
talk, taste, and touch laid down in a collage,
no need for second wind, or second-guessing.
Ô, j'étais sage, et j'en serai en plus,
I promise, and I promise to recover
my equilibrium, my sense of humor,
not let the friend be silenced by the lover.
(It's either that or lie awake and stew more.)
(I wish that there were only beef to stew.)

So smooth
harsh at
the same
time,
She's been
at this a
long time
already.

Coming Downtown

Lie down beside me if it's good for you.
I only had to see you face-to-face.
I won't stay if you don't want me to.

What is this crap we push each other through
the phone wires, through the length of rainy days?
Lie down beside me if it's good for you.

One last sarcastic curveball, that who threw
at whom, and who got stranded on third base?
I won't stay if you don't want me to,

but you didn't show up after, and I knew
a whole night might let wolves loose in our space.
Lie down beside me if it's good for you.

There'll be a cab on Second Avenue.
I'll have the driver bring me to your place.
I won't stay if you don't want me to

—but seeing you illuminates the true
path (for me) through the whole beast-ridden maze.
Lie down beside me if it's good for you

to hold me now. Another night will do
as well (I guess). Though what I'm feeling stays,
I won't stay unless you want me to . . .

A nightcap, or a quick "Afore ye go"?
I need to know my need is no disgrace.
Lie down beside me if it's good for you.

But we avoided that scenario.
A sense of humor is a state of grace,
And I will stay, and I am going to
lie down beside you and be good for you.

IV

Five-thirty, little one, already light
outside. From Spanish Harlem, sun spills through
the seamless windows of my Gauloise blue
bedroom, where you're sleeping, with what freight
of dreams. Blue boat, blue boat, I'll navigate
and pilot, this dawn-watch. There's someone who
is dying, darling, and that's always true
though skin on skin we would obliterate
the fact, and mouth on mouth alive have come
to something like the equilibrium
of a light skiff on not-quite-tidal waves.
And aren't we, when we are on dry land
(with shaky sea legs) walking hand in hand
(often enough) reading the lines on graves?

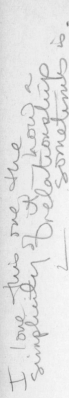

Sometimes, when you're asleep, I want to do
it to myself while I'm watching you. It
would be easy, two fingers along my clit,
back, in, back out. Your skin's heat comes into
me, adjacent. Through the mussed chrysanthemum
petals, your big child's sleep-face, closed around
its openness, gives me your mouth to ground
on, but only with my eyes. I could come
like that, but I don't—take you against your will,
it seems like, and I wouldn't; rather wait
adrowse in sunlight with this morning heat
condensing, a soft cloud above my groin
gently diffusing brightness there, until
you wake up, and you bring it down like rain.

Conversation in the Park

"Do people look at me and know I'm gay?
It's not a problem you would have, because
only a girl goes down the stairs that way,

one at a time, and pigeon-toed. I'm splay-
footed, and I walk like a workhorse
—do people look at me and know I'm gay?"

"What you've got's *style!* Androgyny's passé
—you're all at once tough and voluptuous.
A girl only goes down the stairs that way

with two inside breast pockets, and the key
to a new BMW . . ." "Less prose!
Do people look at me and know I'm gay?"

"The uniform of the politically
correct, dear, would be grounds for a divorce!"
"Only—a girl gets down! The stares—that way

my back aches when I wonder what they say
behind it . . . But you wouldn't know. You *chose!*"
"Do people look at *me* and know I'm gay?"

"Honey, you look like a twelve-year-old boy.
But you go down on me the way, God knows,
only a girl goes down!" "The stairs! That way

out of the park, or else I'm going to lay
you right here, right now, on the grass!" "Yes, boss!
Do people look at us and know we're gay?"
"Why *would* two girls go down the stairs this way?"

Sunday again, dear Julie. Ray was hung
over, inclined to stay in bed and pout.
The clouds came in after the sun came out,
and I was sure my morning cough was lung
cancer, but only one can come unstrung
at a time. "Get up, then. Write about
it if you're scared. Theme: Existential Doubt."
(Sometimes I can pull rank because she's young.)
When I'd typed some and made my coffee, she
had notebook, feet up on the library
desk. I brought her tea and let her be
until, later, she came for me in
the wing chair. That sounds like not what I mean.
I mean, we made the day. Love, Marilyn.

Having Kittens About Having Babies I

Imagine this: You're straight, and I'm a guy.
I have a kid, and I'm older than you.
We love each other, just the way we do.
You want your own child, eventually.
We're great in bed. I'm adequately virile,
but must say (said the doctor, know thy lumps),
"When she was six, Iva gave me the mumps.
I hate to tell you this, love, but I'm sterile."
Would you say, "Babies come from bodies! I'll
spend a few months fucking a high-school friend
or, failing that, cruise bars and pick up men
until one takes, some spring semester while
you're gone. It never will impinge on us!"
And I'd say, "Sure!" Girl, are you serious?

Having Kittens About Having Babies II

It's not by mumps that I'm disqualified
as child begetter. All the rest's the same.
Entitlement is the name of the game.
We're both entitled not to be beside
any point determining our circle.
There are two readings to the text: because
no law defines this love, we are outlaws.
We're not, each to the other, marginal.
Us, and another child, together? Make
us happen, that's one possibility.
I've done it, so I've got the basics down.
First off, the long haul isn't pregnancy.
Second, we do not need another bloke
to tell you when we can or can't leave town.

Having Kittens About Having Babies III

*key here.
the idea
of the
lesbian.*

They get to make their loves the focal point
of Real Life: last names, trust funds, architecture,
reify them; while we are, they conjecture,
erotic *frissons*, birds of passage, quaint
embellishments in margins. Self-restraint
is failing me, and you, dear heart, suspect your
old trout's about to launch into a lecture.
Give me a serious long kiss. I ain't.
Give me another one. Look what we're mak-
ing, besides love (that has a name to speak).
Its very openness keeps it from harm, or
perhaps it wears our live-nerved skin as armor,
out in the world arranging mountains, nak-
ed as some dream of Cousin William Blake.

Half-a-foot taller, it would seem, and half-
a-gallon savvier: "My Girlfriend's Back!"
Does everyone in the fifth grade wear black
rubber bracelets, leather armbands, skirts mid-calf,
stained sweatshirts with hips ridden by a raf-
fish belt? I had just put away a stack
of laundry, laundry, laundry, some wisecrack
about edible skivvies epigraph
for how I wish I felt instead of tired
and missing you. Iva sniffed out your boots
and hair spray. "It looks like Rachel's moved in!"
"Not quite." (That, this: a runthrough, uninspired
recon flight: drilled, each pilot parachutes
over the hump to the quotidian.)

Myself I said it: write it if you're scared.
Twice (more) now, anxious pleasure made a glutton
of me, hurt you, another day's bad joke, but on
the wide beach afterwards, nerves and also ass bared
in the afterwash, I faced your faced-off flared
anger. Anger's honest—yours is—but what un-
dertow dragged us apart here? No, I'm not on
my feet yet. Wind has howled through the place there'd
always (I thought) be shelter when we'd dared
too much, or not enough, elsewhere. *Ô merde!*
Even angry, you were funny and tender,
("Shit, do I have to walk you through a fight?"),
but I woke at the bottom of the night,
happy, amnesiac, until I stared
into a place with nothing at the center.

Over the hump to the quotidian,
each skirmish advances the campaign.
In Riverside Park, the sun's out again,
and multicolored cohorts of the city, in
their undershirts, lounge in it, looking pretty. In
our two laps, Iva rolled, insolent, plain-
ly blissed out, ears studded with gold, disdain-
ing combs and showers. An obsidian
retriever got your tennis ball. You tried
out the softball gloves downslope from me.
Iva and I catch like girls, but we're O
so pleased to have a Saturday hero
throw us a few. Love, the water is wide,
but we are getting over, *en famille*.

Dear Julie, here's your regular Sunday
news from the front. We're in the park, in shorts.
Like twelve-year-olds who've left their book reports
till the last minute, we've come out to play
lugging our notebooks, so that we can say
we tried. In fact, we're trying out all sorts
of stuff, like dinner out with Iva, sports-
wear heaven, lobsters. We gorged on a tray
of seafood antipasto that reminded
me of those *grandes bouffes* in the Via dei
Marci. Write to me! Are you okay?
Iva asked Ray to plug for a TV
for her while she was "doing it" with me.
It didn't work. Here's love—I've sealed and signed it.

so funny!
the presence
of Iva
makes the
whole book
ethically
magnified

Two nights without you is a little much
right through here. Monday fizzled away, though we
talked, and I masterminded two or three
poker hands of plane tickets. You watch
and see, if I have to, I can be butch
in airports, though no way as tough as Érzsi
—with her old friend now in Long Island City.
You'll meet next week. I want our lives to touch
the way our minds do. What our bodies do
together is unprecedented. (Minds
dreamed it up; can the dichotomy.)
Iva's at school. The morning turns and finds
me here, in your pajamas, missing you
between phonecalls and cups of black coffee.

Iva gave us the slip and spent the night
at a school friend's, *imprévu,* so we
had a last-minute girls' night in Chelsea,
tented our love under the skylight,
under the gray sheet, under the cream-white
blankets. Tall kitchen glasses of brandy
washed over everybody's family.
Now we're outlaws with in-laws, who invite
us to meals while the hills call, and rain-slick streets
we'd run at dawn, but don't, turn back to work-
day thoroughfares. My olive skin, your creamy
skin, proclaimed amnesty between heartbeats
for fugitives harried into the dark,
where I see only you, where you can see me.

Yesterday afternoon, I watched my friend
Sonny sleeping in a hospital cub-
icle, face masked, taped to a plastic tube,
while, at a metal table near the end
of the bed, Karyn kept watch. The darkened
room expanded and contracted with
her breathing. I have not stood close to death
often. She coughed, without waking. Karyn
went, whispered to her and massaged her chest,
kissed her forehead, laid down her head on
the place one breast had been, a dozen
years ago. Sonny would say, "Amazon
bodyguard." Between them, on their chosen
proving ground, I kissed both, for you, too, my best.

death comes on the scene.

We won't be in the park today, Julie . . .

Morning of Mother's Day, it's dog weather
in May, in May in which one warrior
fell. I'm going to be a pallbearer
at noon, Julie, stand up with her daughter.
Iva will be there. Ray will be with her.
She fought, and then she told her own story; or-
dinary women can. Old friends, we were
scrappy, sometimes (a pair of stubborn feather-
weights, sparring) but we disagreed like kin.
Heroes converge. Érzsi is coming in
on Tuesday, and my own love walks me through
hangovers, death, and taxes like a scout
leader. We won't be able to cool out
in the park; still, Sundays we think of you.

How can you love me with the things I feel
that scare me crashing on the window glass?
How can you love me when I'm such an ass-
hole (sometimes) I can't take hold of what's real-
ly there and use it, let you take the wheel
and put my head back as the truck-stops pass?
Where would we go that morning? Would the grass
beside the highway mount to granite, steel
and rubber take us far enough that I
could pull my ghosts out of my guts and cry
for them, with you behind me, on some high
stone place, where water breaks from underground
arteries with hard breaths, that would sound
like mine, letting them go, saying good-bye?

V

Last night we kissed as if we hadn't kissed
for weeks. It was two days, but in-between-
times a cast of thousands intervened
with the whole tragicomic shopping list
to be checked off. When you whispered, "I missed
you," I first thought, like you'd missed a train.
Then the song was "She's Back In My Arms Again,"
with catching-up time after, in a mist
of brandy fumes and cigarette smoke. Look
at all these pictures! Here's our back-up group
(the class), you airing your looseleaf notebook
in the park in shades, Iva and me
in Paris being nuts over the soup,
and Budapest in 1943.

In Budapest in 1943,
Érzsi and her pretty journalist
friend, who topped the Nazis' wanted list
sooner, smile at each other on a windy
hill, under an arch, in spy-movie
suits with shoulder pads. She has one fist
raised in this one, Party salute. The dist-
ance between these points: my history
laid across theirs. The blonde knew when to split,
and did. She writes long letters now from Queens
to Érzsi, book-bound on the Buda side
of the Danube. They weren't the ones who died
—and we wonder, like conscripts in their teens,
would we be heroes if things came to it?

You did say, need me less and I'll want you more.
I'm still shellshocked at needing anyone,
used to being used to it on my own.
It won't be me out on the tiles till four-
thirty, while you're in bed, willing the door
open with your need. You wanted *her* then,
more. Because you need to, I woke alone
in what's not yet our room, strewn, though, with your
guitar, shoes, notebook, socks, trousers enjambed
with mine. Half the world was sleeping it off
in every other bed under my roof.
I wish I had a roof over my bed
to pull down on my head when I feel damned
by wanting you so much it looks like need.

Ray's getting a haircut on Irving Place.
I showed your letter to her while she waited
for the goop to dry. Julie, I hate it
that you're down, and I can't get on your case
over a dinner table, face to face,
or even phone. I'm glad, at least, you wrote it.
We've had a bitch week, over-peopled, floated
out of focus, couldn't take the pace
from day to day, but now, T.G.I.F.
As much as we want to be left alone,
I wish I could go out and tie one on
with you, or go to market, then play chef.
Your last few lines were fucking elegant.
. . . I wish you all the fucking you might want.

Would we be heroes if things came to it?
We only get to be tough guys in small ways,
in Central Park, on highways or in hallways.
A big word, but we have a claim to it
or, sometimes, need to give that name to it,
especially the harder times, when you're a
tad turned round toward the flip side of bravura
or I've done something sticky, and stuck blame to it.
The sun's out, but a hero needs repose.
I left you rolled up in the blue-and-white
sheets, where I prematurely crashed last night,
while you coped with one hero grown morose.
Achilles hung out in his tent and pouted
until they made the *Iliad* about it.

Grief, and I want to take it up in you;
joy, and I want to spend it all inside
you; fear, and you are the place I can hide.
Courage is what leaves me brave enough to
turn you around and tell you what to do
to me, after. Rivers, and downstream glide
I; we breathe together. You look, or I'd
get scared, but you're watching while you take me through
the deep part, where I find you, where you need
to know I do know where, know how to drive
the point home. Wit: you get the point and flat
statement of a gift of tongues. I get
up, and you get me down, get lost, you lead
me home, or I take you, and we both arrive.

Holy shit!

This is a thing I've never seen in het sex: that needing to know that the other's satisfied, needing to know the other gets there first until it's almost annoying the virtue that wanting so much for another first

The Commissar wore your black baseball hat.
Iva brushed Meg's reddest hair, perched on
the couch where, deepening in afternoon,
we'd tamped and sealed the day. Enormous cat
battened on scraps while the white skylit flat
spun like a mirrored disco ball around
a TV tribute to The Motown Sound.
One night in Advent—a clandestine date—
you asked the DJ for "Tracks of My Tears,"
and "What Becomes of the Broken-Hearted?"
You held my hand; we danced. We had no right
to speak, then, of what we can toast tonight
with Iva, Meg, and Érzsi. Sweetheart, here's
a hopeful glass to follow what we started.

"Hey, look," I'd like to say—but what could I say
to your Botticellian actress friend?
You said, "I don't know how it's going to end,"
to her, of us. She cried; she made you cry.
Between the two of you, you made my day.
Last night, the messed-up sheets were mine, all mine.
Cold sweats and nightmares do it every time.
I'd like it, Rachel, to end when I die
at ninety-seven in the south of France;
to let it, and let us, get good and old
and bad, without a second lead on hold
dressed for the Reconciliation Scene.
Is there some "end" more imminent you mean?
You told me, I'll tell you, "Give peace a chance."

Where can we be quiet? On the tar
beach above Twenty-Third Street, with the sun
setting behind the sweatshops, we found one
oasis where we pitched our tent. The car
(when you're not Driver to the Commissar)
sometimes becomes a silvery cockpit
encapsulating pilot and copilot
beyond ground time, alone between depar-
ture and arrival. Restaurant tables make
adequate islands when they're set for two
(too seldom). Sometimes, when you sing, your voice
is something like a path around a lake.
Sometimes, even, your white room or my blue
one's the sufficient, necessary place.

Until they made the *Iliad* about it,
nobody would have seen a fit of pique
as quintessentially *geste héroïque*.
Is indecision epic? If you doubt it,
look at the texts. Where would they be without it.
She whose mind's made up fast as she'd eat cake
has not got that right stuff of which bards make
heroes. You'll get another back-rub now—did
that help? This is to get you out of bed
—and me as well—across the treacherous
stretch connecting all-that-out-there and us.
All night your nakedness protected me
from nightmares and insomnia. Now we
must suit you up to go and knock them dead.

My old buddies, your brilliant career
and mine, roommate, old lovers, our neurotic
sets of *copines,* your boss, all seem to have got ex-
plicit instructions from the stratosphere
to keep us just at arm's length right through here.
Cross-country flight, the Grand Hotel—but frantic
appointments back-to-back replace romantic
assignations: *boîtes,* baths, bars for queer
girls (we hit one). We check out, we check in,
jerked like a car with bad brakes on these hills,
huddled like foundlings in too big a bed.
Back on the street with street-smarts on, we win
over, at least, Cab Voluble, who said,
"You yuppies must have huge dry-cleaning bills!"

We suit you up to go and knock them dead.
Autonomy's the colophon of this stance:
it means I stand back and you keep your distance;
you keep your socks up and I keep my head.
At least, we try. We can't go back to bed
with morning light and muffins, kiss and kiss—hands
off for the day. If I were one of Wystan's
bardic collegians, in the potting-shed
wintering bulbs while running *qāsídah*
across my brain, I might compose ghazals,
rhyme-linked, interreflective but discrete,
for the odd things and times we get to eat,
for words in crowds at midday, for the star-
burst blazed one night between these neutral walls.

You on the Red-Eye, I did my last lap
after the reading in a brasserie
on Fillmore. Bill defined the glossary
of Spode and drew flatware on the paper *nappe*.
Perine Place was a hairsbreadth on the map
away, where I lived with Link. I thought of loss. Are we
survivors blurred in fern bars and chinoiserie?
I went to Folsom Street for a nightcap
at the one girls' bar on the leather mile
with some new faces, she and he, young, gay.
You were already hundreds of miles away,
eastbound, airborne, taking home my home,
and I was *disponible* for a short while
—call it the "Free Man in Paris" syndrome.

I want this love to be resilient
as crabgrass cracking the interstices
of paving stones until the sidewalks burst. Its ease
is difficulty, rough when crossed, ebullient
in adversity, still new, unruly, int-
ermittently stormy, rolling with June thunder.
We're getting over, rootlings pushing under
ramshackle walls, knocking them down. A brilliant
midsummer sky, cleaner than metaphors,
blazes above the river. We are three
months old since midnight, appropriately
cheered on a French map, then under the sheet.
I lie beside you now, absorbing heat,
light, currents of cool air, the season's, yours.

Forty-two winters had besieged my brow
when you laid siege to my imagination
in a café named for a subway station,
after those weekly seminars. Fall blew
over to winter, winter admitted you
(I had to admit to Nadja and Danda)
first to my thoughts, then to my house, where, fonder
than I knew I was, I first learned how
to listen to the speaker in the song
you made for me. I first wanted to touch
you as you wired my creaky stereo
to your spare turntable. Before too much
time passed, the last slush banks were disappearing. Now
forty-two summers wouldn't be too long.

VI

From you will I be absent as the spring
turns into summer, and the Paris sky
stays twilit until nearly midnight. I
don't want to go, wouldn't want to stay, hoping
the clearer focus of a distancing
lens will show both of us separately
comet trails marking your trajectory
and mine, convergent, or continuing
asymptotes, toward a human finity
of works and days. Last night was a white night,
my arms around you with a burst of words
compressed between your elbows and your knees.
There are none here, so, in the graying light,
I sang you *rossignols* and mockingbirds.

Mother-and-child reunion, outward bound:
we've three seats, window; on two, Iva's snoozing.
I wouldn't mind a modest bit of boozing
to fuel the jump across the herring pond
away, for three weeks, from you. What, beyond
ambivalence and pleasure, am I choosing
to leave behind me? What do I risk losing?
Roissy is not the only solid ground
I want to feel firmly beneath my feet
after those days of distance, for the sake of
easing the coming distance that I'd planned.
Veteran Iva sportscasted the takeoff,
informed me that she wouldn't want to eat,
and settled in. She'll sleep until we land.

Three flights up in the rue de Turenne,
Iva and I are homesteading. We claim
as ours what first had someone else's name
in our imaginations. Settling in
is strenuous. What's left looked like a squat.
Though almost every day it's cold and rains, out
we stride like leathernecks and shop our brains out:
a new pine table, a new coffee-pot,
the square French pillows we like, Jax disdained,
maybe a lamp table, a reading lamp,
for your arrival, fan and *sèche-cheveux*.
It doesn't look as much as if we're camp-
ing out. I cooked our first real meal, *lapin
à la moutarde,* for I. and me, *à deux*.

You pull away, and like a rubber-band
connection, something pulls me too close, tens-
ion constant: from this vantage point, makes sense,
seems, even, changeable, with understand-
ing. We're still malleable: land
legs may replace sea legs, difference
between us be welcomed in the present tense.
There's no abyss, just breadth: let it expand.
Meanwhile, I've flown across the herring pond.
You're in Chelsea. We've both got work to do
to work our different ways across the distance
between us: there's resilience, resistance.
Meanwhile, I wake up with a strapping blonde
in bed, but she's eleven, and not you.

Is missing you this much part of the plan,
with morning lusts, one-sided afternoon
conversations, evening meals? Mid-June
is cool and muggy. I'm in the Jardin
du Luxembourg, legs stretched on two iron chairs
between the mannered flower-bed and round
pond, while Iva revisits the playground.
(She's gotten old for tales of wolves and bears
who misbehave the way her elders do.)
It's Sunday in the park, with Japanese
toddlers romping in *broderie anglaise,*
ubiquitous Americans who jog,
the *B.C.B.G.* tanning in the smog,
and these few lines connecting me to you.

Dans un pays qui me ressemble, mon
enfant, ma soeur, the *train de nuit* descends.
We slept stacked in *couchettes* with four young men,
mutual strangers, French, with Walkmen on.
The blinds admit bright sunlight at Toulon.
Young men in droves detrain (is there a war
on?) while I smoke in the corridor.
Broom blooms on girlish hillocks, with the sun
stroking it gold. *"Plus qu'il y a du soleil,*
plus tu souris," Marie smiled at me, years
ago, at the bus stop in Cagnes-sur-Mer.
And though two weeks and the Atlantic still
divide us and there'll be a funeral
tomorrow, sunlight makes me smile today.

Julie and I, with laden baskets, stop
at La Régence for coffee. Almost noon:
the pool will open, market close down soon,
but we've already planned a meal and shopped.
Under the plane trees, stirring a cooled cup,
I tell her that, among the *très riches heures,*
some have been less than easy to endure.
"I want this to work for you! Don't fuck up!
I've had it done to me; I've done it—want
something so much you stifle it. Well, don't!"
The unemployable ephebes of Vence
drift to their daily tables: circumstance
inscribes *their* destiny on this event.
We won't, at least, go stale at La Régence.

The despot whom the hero loved is dead.
Abstracted by State fiat from her large
world, she is reluctantly in charge
—military governor, or head-
mistress—of Balkans, boarding school, or bed-
and-breakfast. She came through the war, the purge,
safe in her skin; but now, a demiurge,
restless at ninety-two, rattles her head,
and she tries on the high old style, compares
my friend, her dead friend's daughter, to King Lear's
two eldest, as if this twelve-acre hot-
house were a fiefdom. From it, she'll escort
ashes to urn, cut her possession short.
Despots are petty-minded; heroes, not.

I'm sorry that she never got to flirt
with you. She would have challenged you to chess
at midnight, she, in long Indian dress,
pouring you whiskey, while she stayed alert
on Evian. Or, while colonists got dirt
under their nails, weeding the kitchen garden,
she'd have told you about salons she starred in,
on her Congolese bench, in her Mexican shirt,
while some tired Magyar child prepared the tea;
or spun you in the relic with its gears shot
that she still drove at nearly ninety-three.
Though, to be bad, she might have got around
to asking me, when you were within earshot,
"Whatever happened to the *other* blonde?"

Late one June night while Julie was asleep,
Érzsi and the Countess, drunk as skunks,
came reeling, syncopated by the thunks
of Catherine's backless wedgies on the sheep-
and-goat path the stone steps make, down the steep
olive groves. Julie (in boys' swimming trunks)
was roused out of her solitary bunk's
comforts when pebbles pinged the pane. "What *creep*
is that?" she thought—or thought, "Which boy from town . . ."
and pushed the heavy door out on the dark,
where stood the grinning reprobates—white gown
and navy trousers—quadrilingual drunks,
who hoped she'd join them in a last *vieux marc*.
"Because we're old, we have to live like monks?"

So great! dykes living it up! the lesbos, the woman in these culture in these piece. It shows how we really do make our own familiar how when sex frustration applies to everyone the universally expands or company expands or opens it behaves so much differently

Who's writing up this summer—Graham Greene?
Outside the crematorium for Nice,
old bangers disgorge seven souls apiece.
The horse guard at the pyre of Grande Catherine
sat, baffled, unappeased, on varnished bare
benches, waiting for, at least, a speech
that could have easily been made by each
one there, whether they loved or hated her
or both. Behind her child, I sit between
Julie and Iva. Novel on I.'s knees;
I squeeze Julie's. Something should make us cry—
a requiem in Latin, elegies
in her four languages. Had she forseen
leaving her public waiting when she'd die?

"Whatever happened to the other blonde?"
is what, in different words, Marie once asked,
meaning that Alice seemed to make a fast
assisted exit from your story: bond
insoluble cut quickly. I'd be found
something less than consistent if I passed
over noting, first, that she was last
heard from, unruffled, coupled with astound-
ing speed with somebody whose name (not gender)
mirrors yours, who (she said) didn't know
who and what you were to her. She'd packed
and left. First, you made love. You told me so.
You've told me, so we both know, that you send her
daily, in mind, away—but she comes back.

What's happened to your letters? Is the mail
clerk in love with you and hoarding them
to read, herself, in bed at 5 AM?
I would, if I had got them, on those *gueule
de bois* nights when, before the sky turns pale,
I wake up, fidget, itch, scratch, turn and squirm
and think of every pungent synonym
for "asshole"—who should know not to regale
herself with that much wine, and then turn in
so early, and alone (or, alternate-
ly, drink so much and then stay up so late).
Cockcrow: dogs bark, mist grays the trees beyond
the river. Since I lack the correspond-
ent here, I'd like to have those letters then.

Lacoste V

My imagination tells lies, too.
Crunching the twilit gravel past the vine-
yards, I'm half ripening with them, half in
a Sunday evening colloquy with you.
On scrub-snarled bluffs, village walls are in view
in late-come sunlight for the Fête Saint-Jean.
At midnight, local boys will jump the bon-
fires, some stalwart girls among them who
have got *culot* although they don't have *couilles*.
(It won't be Iva, and it won't be me.)
Beneath the rafters on Midsummer's Eve,
I lay in that wide bed, stretched to believe
we'll be there when we can, walk in the light
of the Midi, constellate summer nights.

I stayed in bed this morning until nine.
I woke at seven—I hadn't quite slept
off last night's wine. Thinking about you kept
me occupied a while. The bed was mine
again. Iva, Unaccompanied Min-
or, went to the airport, inadept-
ly with *my* ticket, so we were re-schlepped
to the Marais and back by a front-line
veteran cabdriver. *"N'inquietez-vous
pas, mesdames!"* and damn, he got us through
with five minutes to spare. He drove like you
said Iva; and then she was gone. *"Une bise!"*
to last me till September. With Annie's
company, the evening went. Reprise:

I'll stay in bed with you, till when, soon, please.

I'll stay in bed with you, but when? Soon, please
let me lie down beside you as the dark,
studded by Broadway windows, headlights, park
lights, touches your shoulders with the breeze.
In P'town, Kim and Jax are having *crises,*
and want us there for back up: a hotel
room may have to do, *en plein bordel.*
That's next week, though.
                 We're in different countries,
still, and your bedtime call is my *reveil.*
I feel sad afterwards, for no good reason.
I love your voice; you're honest. It will pass.
(There's Iva—I get touchy after *she's* gone.)
You'll get up (since your mom's in town) while, say,
I'm having one in the café *d'en face.*

I'm having one in the café *d'en face*
with my string bag of marketing. It's warm
today, for the first time. I'm in bad form
from three weeks' overeating. In the Place
des Vosges, summer's conducted hordes convene.
Half the pedestrians have *Guides Michelin.*
(I shouldn't be having this *pain aux raisins.*)
A tan trio of punked-out European
Young sit down—this lot is speaking Dutch.
As if you slept one off at home, along
the rows of stalls at Sunday morning market
I picked too many peaches, a less-strong
Cantal you'd like. I'll take books to the park—it
is a fine day. I miss you very much.

It's Monday, and I miss you very much.
Too late for letters: four of mine were lost,
you said, and never reached you. If the post ‖
office isn't communication's touch-
stone, what is? <u>I wrote four sitting here</u>
<u>in the *troisième*, waiting for it to rain</u>.
I wrote one half at the pool, half on the train
we caught for Montpellier at Cagnes-sur-Mer;
mailed it, and one more, in Clermont-l'Hérault.
In the Marais, yours waited for us:
you at my kitchen table with a steak,
drink, notebook; you on the crosstown bus;
you, stretching through the weekends with elbow
⌈room for yourself you're learning how to make.⌉

Room for yourself: you're learning how to make
some; sometimes I feel, well, grown up on.
Just don't outgrow me. Transatlantic phone-
call two days ago (I want to wake
up to your voice, much closer) served to break
some silences. Love, I'd already known
you still need four miles, Chelsea, Meg, your own
address. I hope for "ours" one day, but take
your time. That's ours also. It's Monday night.
A leftover roast quail, salad, bread, wine,
will be my meal, *chez moi,* alone. I'll write
to Julie, Iva, write *tout court.* Near nine
sunlight still glints the glass *en face*—a good
evening to stroll around the neighborhood.

And when I stroll around the neighborhood,
and when I sunbathe (now, with wicker basket
of books) in the Place des Vosges, I only ask it
be soon, that we're back together, that my good
places, and yours, be ours, knocking on wood
that you and I are equal to the task it
will present to live well, to amass kit-
chen pleasures, friends, rooms, work (our bed-
time's the same, but sweetheart, you're no angel
in the morning, while I'm the Block Patrol).
This afternoon, it seems within our range. Till
the schoolboys seize the park, I'll read and tan.
I'm limited to handwriting my whole
last day in France—my typewriter's *en panne*.

Last day in France: my typewriter's *en panne,*
hauled for mending to the Porte de Versailles
where it will languish for three weeks, while I
make love to you as often as I can.
Julie's enthralled with a Hungarian,
who wants her to move in after four days
of second-language courtship (French). Always
is a long word I can pronounce. I plan
to start tomorrow night. Not that I'd stopped.
Tomorrow night, I plan to start on top
and get there slowly, following the line
of dark hairs down your belly . . . Or the back
way, spine's keys pressed. Be good, I'll let you make
me stay in bed next morning until nine.

VII

Locked plane and screaming babies—Maleboge
of luggage-handlers' strike, no end in sight.
I might be halfway back to you. I might
be reading Stendhal in the Place des Vosges.
Think of Greek claustrophobes inside the Troj-
an Horse—that's how I feel, rigged out to fight
with champions, fearing phantoms. Will this flight
render me fragile? Wedgwood, Spode, Limoges . . .
Painted and precious?
                              Later: we'd be just
landing, if we'd taken off on time.
Along with every other appetite,
anxiety is neutralizing lust;
last night I could have specified what I'm
(lovingly) going to do to you tonight.

Dear Julie, Provincetown is not Antibes:
we have to keep our tops on at the beach.
Our friends have outings planned for us for each
hour of the day and night, till we're enfeeb-
led by the effort that it takes to get,
oh, just two hours out on the guest-house lawn
alone, keep our mouths shut, feet on a sawn-
off worn wood table, with a cigarette,
a can of Coke. (We're cutting down on booze.
As usual, as soon as I got home,
we got untied, and then we tied one on,
and laughed a lot, and gave our fans a class
act; but the aftermath was *dégueulasse*.)
We've what we had, and more. That's the good news.

Some nights there blazes on these neutral walls
my favorite home movie, starring you.
(When neither of *us* are, it's a deep blue,
triple-X rated—that's for kisses.) All's
well that begins well, talking in the dark
around a brandy. When you're on your back,
your voice gets lower, aphrodisiac
—too bad if we're sprawled in Riverside Park,
but now we're not, and, soon enough, your mouth,
close to my ear, moves over mine, and I
move over you. You say you can't slow-dance;
I say I'm clumsy: not by circumstant-
ial evidence. Everything migrates south
where summer stars burn stories on the sky.

While you slept, I'd pull on, quietly,
jeans and shirt, jacket, take books and go
downstairs (behind her door, Mrs. Aho
was ironing, with the 8 AM TV
news on, low volume), creak through the screen door
and walk off like a sailor in the fog.
No one was on the street but a tan dog
patrolling hedges. The grocery store
was shut. Down toward the bay, Commercial Street
glistened like an abandoned movie set.
A few fag jocks jogged by in shorts. The fleet
was out since dawn. I knew where I could get
coffee, read, chat in French if I wanted to.
Toward ten, town waking, I'd walk back to you.

Three weeks in mid-Manhattan mid-July,
Julie, is a different experience
from rusticating in the South of France
or holing up at artists' colonies.
New Yorkers aren't Parisians, though; they stay
put for the most part: they don't have the chance
to shun the city summer; flee weekends.
(Their offices are all *climatisés*.)
So we've become weekend adventurers
on trains and ferryboats and DC3s.
The salt of the Atlantic's on my skin
and Ray's—we lick it off each other. She's
red-gold, I'm brown. The wind's breath's salty, hers
is sweet, till Monday on the streets again.

Black coffee solo while the fog burns off
the harbor—on Block Island it's Bastille
Day come round as we wake up to real
time from the luscious fantasies we both
fed on in winter, felt fattened enough
to wait out lean weeks, make first fruits a meal
sufficient to the nights. Summer's a heal-
ing time, sometimes. Food grows on trees. You slough
off habits, poisons, till your eyes are clear
as the sky will be later this morning.
What they see sometimes are scabs and scars
on my thin hide. Not always a forgiving
gaze; but we both needed to be here.
The dock's fogged where we stretched out under stars.

While summer stars burn stories on the sky,
we pick the threads to keep weaving our own
eye-straining daily handiwork of grown
women who choose and change, Demand of me
my best (you are). Lover of history,
you know, with Yeats, that chance and choice can luck-
ily cross for more than a good fuck.
Step back: the pattern in the tapestry
won't tell itself till more of it is made.
Although it's eighty-seven in the shade,
we have to work this hard making the hist-
ory we need till, trusting it, we're free
to kiss each other better than when we
imagined kissing when we hadn't kissed.

VIII

Estival Passage

1. This time we've come three thousand miles together
   across the ocean, up the wooden stairs
   concave with two hundred and fifty years
   of footsteps. Late July's uncertain weather
   allows us to relax into each other,
   into this place, this time—and if it scares
   you sometimes that the world's so ancient, there's
   our own time to slip out of time. Your father
   rewarded you for bravery. You shoulder
   your way into a wider place. I can
   see that piratical Jew businessman
   dressed up in so much girl, claiming the older
   world back he'd left behind, while our feet wear
   new episodes into the slanted stairs.

2. New episodes wore down the slanted stairs
   where Iva's thuds had vexed Mme. Voisine.
   If she'd peered out (she did), she might have seen
   us hugging in the corridor, my bare
   feet muddy from the quai, where, *en plein air,*
   en pleine lune, we sang like seventeen-
   year-olds. You brought my book down for Nadine
   at "Le Fandango," who was taking care
   of our wine, your French, that the meal was served
   when our important notebook had been shut.
   By some lopsided schedule we observed,
   we dined at ten, made love at noon; we wrote
   or shopped at seven—thus, your winter coat;
   at two AM, we built a model boat.

3. At two AM, we built a model boat;
   at least, we started one. Each plastic bit
   was smaller than the last. We could admit
   fatigue, at last, pour brandy, let it float
   off to another day. We looked at maps
   in bed, while I leaned back between your breasts.
   We have another home, you said—our masts
   rigged out for voyages. Afternoon naps
   to cure your cold refueled you at three-
   thirty. Lamp extinguished, cars below
   the window heading home, we made it home
   again. No tidal waves, only the foam
   of ancient oceans laved our sleep. You know
   where you'll come if you come back to me.

4. Clouds Thursday, sunny Friday, Saturday
   wind, Sunday it's raining, and you're gone.
   A new book, coffee, warm blueberry scones
   to dip, reading, at "La Fourmi Ailée"
   bookshop, in the lamplit *salon de thé*
   behind the shelves. An afternoon alone:
   tonight starts weeks. *Une extrême attention*
   is the book's title, is what I will pay
   my way back to resume my single self
   walking my work up daily hills down south.
   Low-voiced lovers conspire over poached eggs.
   I lick my crumbs, admire the rainbow shelf
   of teapots, square oak tables with spooled legs
   I'd lean across and, quickly, kiss your mouth.

5. If you come back to me, perhaps you'll come
    out on this rocky ledge wind-strewn with pine
    needles, overlooking a ravine
    grown full of scrub oak, blackberries, and broom.
    I've been sitting out here all afternoon,
    almost naked, mesmerized by green
    leaves turning in the wind, half brilliantined
    by sunlight, half in shadow. There's a hum
    of mowers far away; mostly I hear
    only the sough of Mistral in the trees.
    We could see the Mediterranean
    from the road today, the sky's so clear.
    No one comes by. The rock wall makes a screen.
    (I don't bother to go inside to pee.)

6. I don't bother to go inside to pee.
   We wouldn't have to go indoors to do
   other things, either. I'd lie next to you,
   eyes closed, knee up, bent out against your knee.
   New heat, not solar, would gradually
   course where we touched, suffuse us, going through
   the wires more quickly than a *petit bleu*
   would be delivered by the P.T.T.
   in the old days, when you could send such things.
   Then hands, deliberate, up here, then down.
   Then there'd be words, and noises; they'd be drowned
   by the cicadas' serenade for wings.
   And thus, an afternoon in Vence. This minute,
   perhaps, you're in my bed—but *I'm* not in it.

7. Perhaps, right now, you're sleeping in my bed
over Broadway, ten floors above the street,
hugging the pillow, flowered oversheet
wadded between your knees. Six hours ahead
of you, I make a shopping list: cheese, bread,
paper napkins, maybe something sweet
(tarte aux groseilles?) to share. I'm going to eat
outdoors, with Julie and her friend, instead
of indoors, talking to the typewriter
beside my glass, while you brainstorm for pay.
(Six from nine is three; six from three is nine
on clock faces.) I'll travel back in time
part of a day to find you again, Ray,
if you don't come flying into the future.

8. If you don't come flying into the future,
    where will I meet you? Thursday-before-last
    (now telescoping quickly with "the past")
    when shopping for provisions was adventure,
    and you were first persuaded to present your
    neonate French for *baptême* with *"punaises"*?
    "Une bise!" need not be followed by *on baise,*
    but was. Though where I'll feel it again's moot, your
    adjacent warmth's still what I crave: outdoors
    in some park, with some queen's biography;
    with your guitar, late, on my library
    floor, winding new bronze around the pegs.
    I'd like to throw my laundry in with yours.
    I'd like to put my face between your legs.

9. I'd like to put my face between your legs,
   lick you, my fingers in you, till you moan
   —then stop, so that imperative voice begs
   me, like a child, to finish. On my own
   my fantasies get more perverse than that,
   not what I'd tell you on the telephone
   from Julie's lover's sunlit council flat
   at three o'clock on Tuesday afternoon.
   I'll talk about the mountains and the food,
   say I've remembered how to live alone,
   ask after Meg, remind you that you should
   send poems to magazines, tell you I've shown
   some to Julie. "Come back!" "Come home *soon!*"
   Then, swollen ocean over the dial tone.

10. Now, swollen ocean over the dial tone
    puts paid, each five days, to our colloquies.
    I'd much prefer a check I'd pay with VIS-
    A, drink up, leave the restaurant, amble home,
    hand brushing yours, down some dark but well-known
    street. (When I kiss you, I don't care who sees.)
    I'll make your airport quip, "Be Japanese!"
    mean: use what's given. Given weeks alone,
    use solitude. Pine scents the air. I gather
    the first blackberries when I walk to town.
    My wind's good. Save one stripe. I'm reddish brown.
    I'm, after all, just where I wanted to
    be. If I can't give this "given" to you,
    I'll bring you what I can when we're together.

It was the best week ever, but . . .

Remind me of what's coming, not what's past.
I've got five closets full of souvenirs:
secondhand shirts and linens I amassed.

in Languedoc last summer, Iva's cast-
off bluejeans (the French dress she wore two years
reminds me of what's coming, not what's past),

Raggedy Ann, some Lincoln Logs, a vast
stuffed lion, one stretch-suit from Mothercare,
secondhand shirts and linens I amassed

when she was new in London. There's bombast-
ic Berlioz her dad abandoned there.
Remind me of what's coming, not what's past.

I guess you know, although you haven't asked,
if ever you need shelf space, it's to spare:
secondhand shirts and linens I've amassed

can be culled through, a closet emptied fast
for your chiaroscuro winter gear.
Remind me of what's coming, not what's past—

though we need both: our two fall birthdays, last
week in Paris, Sundays when we wear
secondhand shirts, and linens we've amassed

get rumpled by our matinal bareassed
pastimes, while our private jokes, our queer
secondhand shirts, and linens we've amassed
remind us of what's coming, by what's past.

La Loubiane

Two long-haired women in the restaurant
caress each other's forearms. I avert
my eyes. I'm glad to see them there; I hurt
looking on, lonely, when I so much want
to touch your arm, your hand like that, in front
of two *mémés* enjoying their dessert,
a British couple with two kids, alert
their girls are pigging *frites,* and me. I can't,
and wouldn't, let them know: I'm one; it makes
my thoughts real when they touch each other. They're
guests at the hotel. They go in through
the glassed-in terrace, slow upstairs, to view
the moon go down through snarled vines of their hair.
The little English girls devour their cakes.

Dear Jule, Pick up two bottles of Faugères,
pack up some choice *fripes,* underwear, a rain
jacket, and come north with me on the train
to spend a few days *en célibataires*
in Paris—since there is a *pied-à-terre*
three flights up in the rue de Turenne—
before we both try life *à deux* again
with difficult divergent *partenaires:*
mine, who is absent; yours, who's so much present
you've got to file a claim to make a mess
on a bathroom shelf. He is precise;
she is headstrong. Single blessedness
was not, in retrospect, always unpleasant;
a brief reprise in Paris might be nice.

Letter on August 15

Warm wind tumbles the washing on the line,
blow-drying it at twice a dryer's speed.
    I'm here; you're not.
If no one made this maxim up, it's mine:
    The less you have, the less you need.
Nobody misses what they haven't got

a clue to. (I've never longed for a car,
and the Vençois don't miss a laundromat.)
    I long for you
the livelong day, and all night long. You are
    I know, worth going on about
—knowledge which, at the moment, doesn't do

me any good. Someone who's lifted weights
for months, then quits, finds that sinuous force
    soon turns to flab.
My fiber's sagging now. Back in the States
    you miss me too. That makes it worse.
You'd drop downstairs by twos and hail a cab

and come uptown, if I were home uptown.
More prudently, I'd take the bus to Nice's
    flower-bed airport,
wave from the deck while the Airbus touched down,
    then, there you'd be. Now the breeze is
transmitting a late-afternoon report

of birdshot on the bluffs of the Malvan,
with cries of men and dogs, and (elsewhere) babies.
    Assumption Day
had morning market, so good mothers can
    lay out the feast. Not risen, they, dec-
ently clad, brought extra francs to pay.

for a tall, thin white candle or a squat
one in a cup, this morning, before Mass.
    In Paris, you
lit them, twice, for your father, joking that
    Mary was tolerant, would pass
over, quicker than he, your bad Hebrew.

I lit one for my mother, awkwardly,
today—the squat kind; I'm more used to tapers—
    and thought of her,
Sonny Wainwright, and Catherine Karolyi.
    At the Régence, with newspapers
in French and English, I fancied you were

feeding me crossword clues from the *Tribune,*
saying my sugarless *citrons pressés*
    were *dégueulasses.*
I walked back to my hermitage at noon,
    washed out some shirts, and spent the day's
hot hours under the pine trees where the grass

under their fragrant sheddings can't grow much.
I sat on a straw beach-mat with James Wright
    and the blue sky,
and, salted down with sweat, wished I could touch
    you now with words, that cooler night
breezes would touch us both, that there'd be eye

contact and talk across a dinner table.
You might not like the half-mile walk uphill
    to restaurants,
shops and cafés. One day, I may be able
    to smile as you appraise the vil-
las and old-age pensioners of Vence.

I imagine your one, Florida mother
drinking pastis here, midday, with her peers,
    gilt middle-class
emigrées. In New Jersey, the other,
    who's seen you once, in twenty years,
may have thought about you today at Mass,

as I did, without sacraments, your rings'
unspecified contract on my left hand
    meaning as big, or
as small, a thing as how we'll manage things.
    Your large soul's from that Jewish man;
that Irish woman fueled its hybrid vigor,

then left you knowing just enough to miss
a scent, a texture—where the memory
    lives, you forget.
She is, for ignorance of what she is,
    the obvious banality
of corner boys' most frequent epithet.

Can we fill out each other's family?
My child (missing you can't obliterate
    how I've missed her)
is cagey, but confided in you, she
    had measured out our three birthdates
and liked that you could be her older sister

—which makes me feel like everybody's aunt,
wishing to cast spinsterly ironies on
    my August quandary
of wanting you here with me, where you can't
    be, anyway, not this season.
The sun is dropping. I'll take in the laundry.

O little one, don't make any mistakes!
It shouldn't matter, but it does. You see
her every day; nights too. She's twenty-three
and had all the encouragement it takes
for her infatuation—in set-breaks
on the court, in girls' bars, when her knee
lingers, whether or not you mention me
—to be called love, and love, we both know, makes
its own excuses. Opportunities
follow: did she, last night, "have to sleep over"
again? It's still last night there. Maybe she's
asleep, one muscled leg outside the cover
one bent into the warmth of her new lover,
while your old one frets over thoughts like these.

While your old one frets over thoughts like these,
my young one's taken somewhat better charge
of how her days and thoughts are growing large
with self-defining possibilities:
that's what I wish for you. Your wish for me's
time used, good work. I'm trying to discharge
the task. Remember when we watched a barge
low on the river, tracking New Jersey's
shoreline, toward a bridge you still don't cross?
We were each other's new ones, opening
to what we brought each other, even loss
you'd send downriver; I said, we'd contain.
Knowing your loss, I'll open to your gain.
I have your picture from that day in spring.

Eight Days in August

1.   Mid-August. In an hour, you're calling me
at a phone booth in the middle of
nowhere. Who has got such faith in love
to think it can glide thermals across three
thousand miles of ocean, hawkeyed, see
me on this hill, and plummet to my glove?
The leather hood descends over its ruff.
What will the words strapped to its talon be?
Probably not *"J'arrive!"* "I want you with
me more than ever"'s not the note a myth-
ological bird totes. (I made a late-
afternoon visit, Friday, to the bank,
to make sure that I had enough five-franc
pieces to call you, if you make me wait.)

2.   Then the phone rang. You didn't make me wait
long, sitting on the booth-stoop in the brambles.
Then, unintelligible static, scrambled
by the transatlantic cable, bait
for my coin's clank, attempting to call back.
Connection made at last, O love, your voice
caressed one ear; the other filtered noise
of locusts, magpies, builders past the black-
berry bushes blighting with bungalows
the stubborn slopes beside the crooked path
down to the crooked house the notary
sealed up with wax and ribbon after Cath-
erine died. Wires out of nowhere link us. We
hold on too long, till one cuts short and goes.

3.   One cuts short and goes. The other goes
uphill, past Saint Anne's chapel, then halfway
up the switchbacks that mount to Saint-Jeannet.
Above, villas, the perched village. Below's
round Vence, in the enceinte it overflows
now, down toward Cagnes-sur-Mer, up toward the gray
moonscape of the Col, up toward the clay-
red stain fireplanes flung on the flaming Baous.
Each one has gone back to the thing she knows
best, for a while, at least, until it changes.
Down to the hidden river, tangled range is
marked to be sliced by land developers;
though change can, too, mean joinings: "hers" and "hers"
connect, in what gets wilder as it grows.

4.   Connecting what gets wilder as it grows
with what's safe, known, quotidian, routine
and necessary as pairs of old jeans
we each wear three times weekly, will be those
new months' task, or, I hope it will, suppose
you want what I want. Love, I want the wild
things now, the rampant undergrowth. Wild fig-
trees' fruit empurples near the road. The moon
swells every night, while underneath one tiled
roof, one restless woman, out of cig-
arettes, wants you, and counts out *"Une semaine,
trois jours,"* and counts once more, to ascertain
that's right, and wouldn't cry, just blows her nose
again (the pollen), "In ten days, that's soon."

5. Fall in September, in ten days. That's soon
    to think of summer gone. Through the café's
    sprawl on the *place,* I notice the *planiers'*
    dry leaves, after a wind, in brown heaps, strewn
    beneath the wrought-iron chairs and dented tin
    tables. Julie and I have a gray day's
    six o'clock drinks in front of us. She says
    she's more than half unsettled, settled in
    somebody else's rooms all through the hot
    afternoons. Jobless Algerian
    wives squabble in the courtyard, while she paces
    and smokes, and thinks of places she is not.
    We severally deplore our states of stasis,
    talk shop, part, and go back to them again.

6.   I shop, in part, just to go back again
to where I was when I was here before.
The fish man hailed Marie and me: *"Bonjour
M'sieu'dame,"*—I was *"Monsieur."* With Kim
(or Iva) though, he read me as *"Madame,"*
"Madame," through solitary months spent more
or less content. The adequate bookstore
sells videotapes now, instead. The tan
honey-blonde *fripe* lady takes August off;
but Alpine honey, newly bottled in
preserve jars, comes in August *(romarin,
lavande)* in the truck-farmers' corner of
the market. There are no more carraway
biscuits. Today was my last market day.

7. Bisque-baked Friday was my last market day
of the season, but I only bought
raspberries and bread, and was, in thought,
the usual three thousand miles away,
and stopped, as usual, at the café,
and told myself, as usual, I ought
to live the days I'm living, till I caught
myself inventing dialogue: the play
a phone booth drama, Traveler's Return,
or what-if-I-walked-home-and-found-you-there.
Enough! I crushed one more tart raspberry
on my tongue; left town. Sunday, the air
is storm-laden. Less mountainside will burn
this August. In an hour you're calling me.

Coda

Maybe it was jet lag, maybe not,
but I was smoking in the kitchen: six,
barely, still dark: beyond the panes, a mix
of summer storm and autumn wind. I got
back to you; have I got you back? What
warmed me wasn't coffee, it was our
revivified combustion. In an hour,
gray morning, but I'd gone back to my spot
beside you, sleeping, where we'd stayed awake
past exhaustion, talking, after, through
the weeks apart, divergent times and faces.
I fell asleep, skin to warm skin, at daybreak.
Your breasts, thighs, shoulders, mouth, voice, are the places
I live, whether or not I live with you.

Fog hid the road. The wipers shoved back torrents
across the windshield. You, on knife-edge, kept
driving. Iva, in the back seat, wept
histrionically. The crosscurrents
shivered like heat-lightning into the parent's
shotgun seat. I shut up, inadept
at deflecting them. A Buick crept
ahead at twenty-five an hour. "Why aren't
we passing him? My Coke spilled. The seat's wet.
You guys keep whispering so I can't hear."
"Sit in the front with us, then."
                              "No! I'll get
too hot. Is the fan on? What time is it?
What time will it be when we get there?"
Time to be somewhere else than where we are.

"What do we have? I guess we still don't know."
I was afraid to say, you made me feel
my sectioned heart, quiescent loins, and spill
past boundaries the way blackberry-brambles grow
up those tenacious hills I left for you.
Their gritty fruit's ripe now, but oceans still
separate us, waves opaque as oatmeal,
miles of fog roiling between your pillow
and mine while you say your best: sometimes, she's where
your compass points, despite you, though a meal
with me, or talk, is good . . . Where our starfire
translated depths, low fog won't let you steer
by sight. The needle fingers one desire,
and no other direction can compel.

If no other direction can compel *a*
me upward from the dark-before-the-dawn *b*
descending spiral, I drop like a stone *b*
flung into some scummed-over stagnant well. *a*
The same momentum with which once we fell *a*
across each other's skies, meteors drawn *b*
by lodestones taproots clutched in unmapped ground
propels me toward some amphibious hell *a*
where kissing's finished, and I tell, tell, tell *a*
reasons as thick and sticky as frogspawn: *b*
had I done this, that wouldn't have come undone. *b*
The wolf of wolf's hour cried at once too often
picks out enfeebled stragglers by the smell *a*
of pond scum drying on them in the sun. *b*

amazing re-use of rhymes. no enjambment. no verbal complexity.

I miss you more than when I was in France
and thought I'd soon be done with missing you.
I miss what we'd have made past making do,
haft meshing weft as autumn days advance,
transliterating variegated strands
of silk, hemp, ribbon, flax, into some new
texture. I missed out on misconstrued
misgivings; did I miss my cue; boat? Chanc-
es are, the answer's missing too. At risk
again, sleep and digestion, while I seize on
pricklier strands, crushed to exude the reason
I can't expect you'll ring up from your desk,
calling me Emer, like Cuchulain's queen,
to say, we need bread and some salad greens.

Cuchulain's lover.

On your birthday, I reread Meredith,
whose life's mean truths inform, tonight, his text
so generously framed. There'll be the next
night, and the next, cold gaps. I'd have been with
you now, lover and friend, across the width
of some candle-lit table as we mixed
habit and hope in toasts. Instead, perplexed
by separation like a monolith
bulked in the rooms and hours I thought would be
ours, I practice insensibility.
We crossed four miles, three thousand. You diminish
now, on a fogged horizon, far away.
Your twenty-fifth was our first class Tuesday
—will one year bracket us from start to finish?

Will one year bracket us from start to finish,
who, in an evening's gallant banter, made
plans for new voyages to span decades
of love and work around a world we'd win? Wish
was overgrown with fears; voyages vanish
with empty wine bottles and summer's paid
bills. Lengthens the legendary blade
between us: silence; hope I hope to banish;
doubt, till I almost doubt what happened, did.
Chicken from Zabar's warms, and frozen spinach
simmers, while Iva writes a school essay:
"Both Sides: Everything has an opposite . . ."
sucking her inky fingers and her braid,
and I read Meredith, on your birthday.

"Why did Ray leave her pipe tobacco here
in the fridge?" Iva asks me while we're
rummaging for mustard and soy sauce
to mix with wine and baste the lamb. "Because
cold keeps it fresh." That isn't what she means,

we both know. I've explained, there were no scenes
or fights, really. We needed time to clear
the air, and think. What she was asking, was,
"Why did Ray leave

her stuff if she's not coming back?" She leans
to extremes, as I might well. String beans
to be sautéed with garlic; then I'll toss
the salad; then we'll eat. (Like menopause
it comes in flashes, more or less severe:
why did you leave?)

"Now that you know you *can,* the city's full
of girls—just notice them! It's not like pull-
ing teeth to flirt," she said, "or make a date."
It's quite like pulling teeth to masturbate
(I didn't say), and so I don't. My nice

dreams are worse than nightmares. As my eyes
open, I know *I* am; that instant, feel
you with me, on me, in me, and you're not.
Now that you know

you don't know, fantasies are more like lies.
They don't fit when I try them on for size.
I guess I can, but can't imagine what
I'd do, with whom, tonight. It's much too late
or soon, so what's yours stays yours. It has until
now. That, you know.

Who would divorce her lover with a phone
call? You did. Like that, it's finished, done—
or is for you. I'm left with closets of
grief (you moved out your things next day). I love
you. I want to make the phone call this
time, say, pack your axe, cab uptown, kiss
me, lots. I'll run a bubble bath; we'll sing
in the tub. We worked for love, loved it. Don't sling
that out with Friday's beer cans, or file-card it
in a drawer of anecdotes: "My Last
Six Girlfriends: How a Girl Acquires a Past."
I've got "What Becomes of the Broken-Hearted"
run on a loop, unwanted leitmotif.
Lust, light, love, life all tumbled into grief.
You closed us off like a parenthesis
and left me knowing just enough to miss.

"Anyone who (I did) ran down Broadway
screaming, or dropped in Bryant Park in a faint
similarly provoked, will sniff a taint
of self-aggrandizement in the assured way
you say: so be it; then she cut the cord; hey,
the young are like that. Put yourself on main-
tenance, stoically, without more complaint?
Grown-ups, at least, will not rush to applaud. They
won't believe you." And he downed his Negroni.
Who wants to know how loss and sorrow hit
me daily in the chest, how like a stone
this bread tastes? Even though lunch is on me,
he doesn't. Home alone is home, alone.
(I'd reach for *Nightwood,* but she "borrowed" it.)

Did you love well what very soon you left?
Come home and take me in your arms and take
away this stomach ache, headache, heartache.
Never so full, I never was bereft
so utterly. The winter evenings drift
dark to the window. Not one word will make
you, where you are, turn in your day, or wake
from your night toward me. The only gift
I got to keep or give is what I've cried,
floodgates let down to mourning for the dead
chances, for the end of being young,
for everyone I loved who really died.
I drank our one year out in brine instead
of honey from the seasons of your tongue.